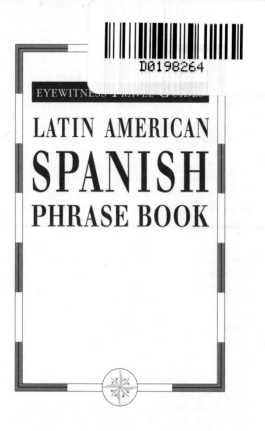

EYEWITNESS TRAVEL GUIDES

LATIN AMERICAN
SPANISH
PHRASE BOOK

DORLING KINDERSLEY
LONDON · NEW YORK · SYDNEY · MOSCOW
www.dk.com

A DORLING KINDERSLEY BOOK

www.dk.com

Compiled by Lexus Ltd with Mike Gonzalez
Printed and bound in Italy by Printer Trento Srl.

First published in Great Britain in 1998
by Dorling Kindersley Limited
9 Henrietta Street, London WC2E 8PS

Copyright 1998, 1999 © Dorling Kindersley Limited, London
2 4 6 8 10 9 7 5 3

A CIP catalogue record is available from the British Library.
ISBN 0 7513 1104 9

Picture Credits

Jacket: special photography DK Studio, Philip Dowel, Dave King,
Neil Mersh; BRITSTOCK - IFA: Erich Bach front centre above;
Chris Cheadle front bottom right; Bernd Ducke front top left;
IMPACT: Peter Menzel back bottom left; Michael Mirecki front
bottom left; NEIL SETCHFIELD: front centre left/centre right,

CONTENTS

PREFACE

This *Eyewitness Travel Guide Phrase Book* has been compiled by experts to meet the general needs of all travellers to those South and Central American countries, Mexico and parts of the Caribbean where Spanish is the principal language. Important characteristics of Latin American Spanish are illustrated in the Introduction, and particular variations in vocabulary and usage are indicated by abbreviated country names throughout the text. In essence, though, the language differs no more from 'European' Spanish than 'American' English does from 'British' English.

Arranged under headings such as Hotels, Driving and so forth, the ample selection of useful words and phrases is supported by a 2,300-line mini-dictionary. There is also an extensive menu guide listing approximately 700 dishes or methods of cooking and presentation. Typical replies to questions you may ask during your journey, and the signs or instructions you may see or hear, are shown in tinted boxes. In the main text, the pronunciation of Spanish words and phrases is imitated in English sound syllables. The Introduction gives basic guidelines to Spanish pronunciation.

The following abbreviations are used in this book for those Latin American countries where Spanish is spoken:

(Arg)	Argentina	*(Cos)*	Costa Rica	*(Mex)*	Mexico
(Bol)	Bolivia	*(Cub)*	Cuba	*(Nic)*	Nicaragua
(CAm)	Central	*(Ecu)*	Ecuador	*(Par)*	Paraguay
	America	*(ElS)*	El Salvador	*(Per)*	Peru
(Chi)	Chile	*(Gua)*	Guatemala	*(Uru)*	Uruguay
(Col)	Colombia	*(Hon)*	Honduras	*(Ven)*	Venezuela

Eyewitness Travel Guides are recognised as the world's best travel guides. Each title features specially commissioned colour photographs, cutaways of major buildings, 3-D aerial views and detailed maps, plus information on sights, events, hotels, restaurants, shopping and entertainment.

PRONUNCIATION

When reading the imitated pronunciation, stress that part which is underlined. Pronounce each syllable as if it formed part of an English word, and you will be understood sufficiently well. Remember the points below, and your pronunciation will be even closer to the correct Spanish.

a	always as in 'back'
g	always hard as in 'get'
H	represents the guttural sound of 'ch' as in the Scottish 'loch' – don't pronounce this as 'lock'
I	pronounced as 'eye'
o	always as in 'hot' (except when as *ow* below)
ow	as in 'cow'
s	always sound the Spanish 's' as a double 'ss' as in 'missing', never like the 's' in 'easy'
y	always as in 'yet', not as in 'why' (e.g. **siento** sy*e*nto)

In the Spanish of Latin America, **z** and **c**, when they come before 'e' or 'i', are pronounced in the same way – like the English 'ss' in 'missing'. Similarly, **v** can be spoken in such a way that it is hard to tell it apart from **b**. The English speaker should pronounce these letters like the English 'v' and 'b'.

There are noticeable differences in the rhythm of speech between one Latin American country and another – the pronounced sing-song of Mexico, for example – but there are few differences in pronunciation between the countries. The main variations are these:

ll and **y** are pronounced 'dj' (as the 'g' sound in 'deluge') in Argentina, Uruguay and Paraguay, and 'y' (as in 'yet') elsewhere. Thus you may hear the word **llave** pronounced *dja*veh or *ya*veh.

In many Latin American countries, the final **s** of a word will not be pronounced. So for **hombres** you may hear *o*mbreh rather than *o*mbress.

In Mexico, Central America and the Caribbean, the **s** is sometimes not pronounced even in the middle of a word.
Thus **piso** might be pronounced *pee-HO* rather than *pee*sso.

GENDERS AND ARTICLES

Spanish has two genders for nouns – masculine and feminine.
In this book, we generally give the definite article ('the') – **el** for masculine nouns, **la** for feminine nouns, **los** for masculine plural nouns and **las** for feminine plural nouns. Where the indefinite article ('a, an') is more appropriate, we have given **un** for masculine nouns and **una** for feminine nouns or the words for 'some', **unos** (masculine) and **unas** (feminine).

USE OF THE WORDS FOR 'YOU' IN LATIN AMERICA

In most of Latin America, if you know someone well, or they are significantly younger, you can address them with the familiar word for 'you' – **tú**. However, in Argentina, Uruguay, Paraguay and Nicaragua, a different familiar form is used – **vos**. When speaking to a stranger or to an older person you don't know well, you should always use the more formal word **Usted**. When addressing more than one person, whether you know them well or not, use the plural **Ustedes**.

BACKGROUND NOTES

Latin America was born out of a bloody encounter between cultures – the Indian culture already existing there and the Spanish seeking to conquer and colonise the continent. Other cultures came later – particularly from Africa which unwillingly gave the slave labour to sustain the sugar plantations of the coastal lands. The variety of cultures is matched by the diversity of landscape on a land mass that embraces high mountain ranges, swamps and rain forests, deserts and high plateaux.

This diversity is reflected in every area of culture. The dominant language is Spanish, but Portuguese, French and English are European languages spoken by large populations. The indigenous languages spoken before the Spanish Conquest are still spoken by millions, though they have also changed and evolved. There is a great diversity of religions, sometimes working with the dominant Catholic religion, sometimes in parallel to it. The range of music played, sung and danced to across the continent is a mixture of rhythms and sounds originating in many different places, just as Latin American food is representative of tastes, methods of preparation and ingredients from innumerable sources.

In the Andean countries of Peru, Bolivia, Colombia and Ecuador the mountain areas embrace many different indigenous communities, such as the Quechua and Aymará Indians. The clothes these people wear reflect a mountain life: warm capes and blankets – **ponchos** *(Per)*, **ruanas** *(Ecu)* – and woollen hats – **chuyos** – to guard against the cold of the Peruvian Andes (**la sierra**) or the high Bolivian plateau (**el altiplano**). In Chile, the southern Mapuche people have begun to organise themselves politically in recent years, having suffered oppression for centuries. Mexico was home to the Aztec empire and the Maya civilisation which occupied Central America before the Spanish came. The remains of both societies are still to be seen, from the pyramids of the ancient cultures of Mexico to the rain forest city states of the Maya which extended from Mexico to Honduras.

The small farms and village communities of the mountains are a dramatic contrast to the great modern estates (**haciendas**) of the coastal areas producing the export crops (coffee, sugar, bananas) on which many Latin American economies still depend.

By contrast Argentina and Uruguay have a strong and obvious European connection and a rather different history. The great cattle ranches and farms (**estancias**) produce the meat and wheat which Argentina exports, and the capital cities of these countries, Buenos Aires and Montevideo, are highly cosmopolitan.

Indeed, it is the cities which dominate each society, drawing the population from the countryside and presenting every aspect of contemporary Latin America. Enormous wealth, displayed in grand houses, exclusive shopping areas, luxury hotels and restaurants, contrasts with the poverty of the shanty towns that surround every major city. Each country has its own name for the shanty towns: **pueblos jóvenes** in Peru, **callampas** in Chile, **ciudades perdidas** in Argentina, **ranchos** in Venezuela. Their inhabitants form part of the 'informal' economy, many of them selling items in the streets (**los ambulantes**) or working casually. The contrast obviously produces social tensions which from time to time explode.

The Catholic Church is a presence everywhere in Latin America, containing as it does over 80% of the world's Catholics. Its churches, cathedrals and monasteries are varied in style and magnificence – though they share a particularly dramatic representation of suffering in their statues and figures. Latin America has also produced the 'theology of liberation', born out of the identification between religions and their local communities, and radical in its tone and activities. Other religions coexist with Catholicism, their origins in the pre-Hispanic world or the beliefs brought from Africa by slaves and kept alive in a dynamic system of worship (**santería**).

The visitor to Latin America will face a sometimes dramatic diversity and contrast. The music will change from the sentimental ballads accompanied by guitars and violins of northern Mexico (**música ranchera**) or the flamboyant trumpeters in silver studded suits of the **mariachi** to the wooden xylophones (**marimbas**) of Central America. The Andes has produced the wooden flutes (**quena**) and panpipes (**zampoña**) now so familiar elsewhere in the world. And Europe has also embraced the dance forms of Latin America from the **tango** of Argentina to the **rumba** born of Cuban folk music and later transformed into the ubiquitous **salsa**. In Latin America, the **cumbia** is the most popular music for dancing.

SOME DO'S AND DON'TS

It is hard to generalise about people's behaviour across so much, and such different, social and physical terrain, but certain features do appear to be common to most Latin Americans. The most obvious is courtesy and formality when people meet. Latin Americans will generally greet those they find in a shop or a bar whether they know them or not. A word and a nod of the head may be enough, but it is important that the visitor should also acknowledge those he encounters.

The same is particularly true in someone's home. You will find that Latin Americans readily invite you into their homes. When you enter a room you should greet the people already there and shake their hand. The visitor should follow the custom and say 'please' and 'thank you' more often than one might in English. In part it is an excess of formality, in part a genuine acknowledgment of the other person.

Naturally enough, if you try to photograph someone without asking their permission they may well protest. Ask their permission first.

Most local people you meet will act with generosity; as always, it seems that the poorest people are the most generous. If you are invited into someone's home and offered food or drink it is churlish to refuse, whether or not you feel they can afford it. It doesn't mean you have to accept everything, but it does mean that you cannot refuse unless you can find a very good excuse.

Generally this courtesy does not extend to punctuality; Latin

Americans can be infuriatingly approximate about all times and you will have to develop a strategy for dealing with everybody's casual timekeeping. Partly it is habit, but partly too that the major cities are so subject to traffic jams and crises that you simply can't tell how long any journey will take.

The other face of Latin America is officialdom, be it the endless bureaucracies or the infinite variety of uniformed personnel. They can be very oppressive, and official institutions are often very hard to penetrate. It is important not to be put off and to insist politely wherever you can. If you know you are going to cross a frontier, and you anticipate problems, dress smartly – it might help.

LOOKING AFTER YOURSELF

Diet is important: eat well and drink lots of bottled or sterilised water – you cannot guarantee clean water supplies in some parts of the continent. Remember that this applies to vegetables, fruit and fresh fruit drinks, all of which will have been washed or made with the same water. So wash them again, and drink from bottles or cans.

Latin American food is spicy; that is its great quality. But it will affect an unaccustomed stomach. So, go prepared with some treatments for an upset stomach and assume your body will get used to the new sensations. Be prepared for the extremes of temperature: the suffocating heat of the sub-tropics (drink plenty of water and protect yourself particularly against the midday sun) and the sudden night cold of the Andes (take warm clothing with you – and sunblock for the daytime!).

USEFUL EVERYDAY PHRASES

Yes/no
Sí/No
see/no

Thank you
Gracias
grass-yass

No, thank you
No, gracias
no grass-yass

Please
Por favor
por fa-vor

I don't understand
No entiendo
no ent-yendo

Do you speak English/French/German?
¿Habla usted inglés/francés/alemán?
abla oosteh eengless/franssess/alleh-man

I can't speak Spanish
No hablo español
no ablo espan-yol

Does anyone here speak English?
¿Hay alguien que habla inglés?
I alg-yen keh abla eengless

I don't know
No sé
no seh

Please speak more slowly
Por favor, hable más lento
por fa-vor ableh mass lento

Please write it down for me
Me lo escribe por favor
meh lo eskreebeh por fa-vor

My name is …
Me llamo …
meh yamo

How do you do? *(hello)*
¿Cómo le va?
komo leh va

Very well, thank you
Muy bien, gracias
moo-ee byen grass-yass

Pleased to meet you
Mucho gusto
mootcho goosto

How are you?
¿Cómo está usted?
komo esta oosteh

Hello!/Hi!
¡Hola!
ola

Good morning
Buenos días
bweh-noss dee-ass

Good evening
Buenas tardes
bweh-nass tardess

Good night
Buenas noches
bweh-nass notchess

Goodbye/See you later
Hasta luego
asta lweh-go

Cheerio!/Bye!
¡Chao!
chow

Excuse me! *(when sneezing etc)*
¡Perdón!
pairdon

(to get attention)
¡Oiga, por favor!
oyga por fa-vor

Excuse me, please *(to get past)*
Con permiso
kon pairmeesso

Sorry!
¡Disculpe!
deesskoolpeh

I'm really sorry
Le ruego me disculpe
leh roo-eh-go meh deesskoolpeh

Can you help me?
¿Me puede ayudar?
meh pweh-deh a-yoodar

Can you tell me …?
¿Puede decirme …?
pweh-deh desseermeh

Can I have …?
¿Me da …?
meh da

I would like …
Quisiera …
keess-y<u>ai</u>ra

Is there … here?
¿Hay … aquí?
I … ak<u>ee</u>

Where can I get …?
¿Dónde consigo …?
d<u>o</u>ndeh kons<u>ee</u>go

How much is it?
¿Cuánto vale?
kw<u>a</u>nto v<u>a</u>leh

What time is it?
¿Qué hora es?
keh <u>o</u>ra ess

What's that?
¿Qué es eso?
keh ess <u>e</u>sso

I've lost my way
Me perdí
meh paird<u>ee</u>

Cheers!
¡Salud!
sal<u>oo</u>

Where is the …?
¿Dónde está el/la …?
d<u>o</u>ndeh est<u>a</u> el/la

Where are the toilets?
¿Dónde están los servicios/baños *(Mex)*?
dondeh estan loss sairveess-yoss/ban-yoss

Go away!
¡Váyase!
vaya-seh

THINGS YOU'LL HEAR

aquí tiene	here you are
¡bien!/¡bueno!	good!
¡buen viaje!	have a good trip!
¿cómo dijo?	pardon?
¿cómo está?/¿cómo le va?	how are you?
¡cuidado!	look out!
de nada	you're welcome, don't mention it
¿de veras?	is that so?
encantado	pleased to meet you
es cierto	that's right
está bien	OK
exacto	exactly
gracias, igualmente	thank you, the same to you
¡hasta luego!	see you later!
¡hola!	hello!, hi!
¡me da mucha pena!	I'm so sorry!
muchas gracias	thank you very much
mucho gusto	nice to meet you
muy bien, gracias	very well, thank you
– ¿y usted?	– and you?
no entiendo	I don't understand
no hay de qué	don't mention it
no sé	I don't know
¡pase!	come in!

→

15

por favor	please
por nada	you're welcome
¿qué dijo?	what did you say?
¿qué hay de nuevo?	what's new?
¿se puede?	may I?
sírvase usted mismo	help yourself

THINGS YOU'LL SEE

abierto	open
agua potable	drinking water
ascensor	lift
aseos	toilets
baños	toilets
caballeros	gents
caja	cashier
calle	street
carretera	road
cerrado (por vacaciones)	closed (for holiday period)
damas	ladies' room
día feriado/festivo	public holiday
elevador	lift
empujar	push
entrada	way in, entrance
entrada gratis/libre	admission free
entre sin llamar	enter without knocking
feriados/festivos	public holidays
halar	pull
hombres	gents
horario/horas de oficina	opening times
horario/horas de visita	visiting hours
información turística	tourist information
laborables	working days
mujeres	ladies' room
ocupado	engaged

→

peligro	danger
precaución	caution
primer piso	ground floor
privado	private
prohibido	prohibited, forbidden
prohibido el paso	no trespassing
recién pintado	wet paint
reservado	reserved
salida	way out
salida de emergencia	emergency exit
se alquila departamento	apartment for rent
se arrienda departamento	apartment for rent
segundo piso	first floor
señoras	ladies' room
se prohíbe la entrada	no admittance
servicios	toilets
se traspasa/se vende	for sale
silencio	silence, quiet
sótano	basement

DAYS, MONTHS, SEASONS

Sunday	domingo	*domeengo*
Monday	lunes	*looness*
Tuesday	martes	*martess*
Wednesday	miércoles	*myairkoless*
Thursday	jueves	*Hweh-vess*
Friday	viernes	*vyairness*
Saturday	sábado	*sabado*
January	enero	*enairo*
February	febrero	*febrairo*
March	marzo	*marsso*
April	abril	*abreel*
May	mayo	*ma-yo*
June	junio	*Hoon-yo*
July	julio	*Hool-yo*
August	agosto	*agosto*
September	septiembre	*set-yembreh*
October	octubre	*oktoobreh*
November	noviembre	*nov-yembreh*
December	diciembre	*deess-yembreh*
Spring	primavera	*preemavaira*
Summer	verano	*vairano*
Autumn	otoño	*oton-yo*
Winter	invierno	*eemb-yairno*
Christmas	Navidad	*naveeda*
Christmas Eve	Nochebuena	*notcheh-bweh-na*
Easter	Pascua, Semana Santa	*paskwa, semana santa*
Good Friday	Viernes Santo	*vyairness santo*
New Year	Año Nuevo	*an-yo nweh-vo*
New Year's Eve	Nochevieja	*notcheh-vyeh-Ha*
Twelfth Night	Reyes	*ray-ess*

NUMBERS

0	cero *sairo*	10	diez *dyess*
1	uno, una* *oono, oona*	11	once *onsseh*
2	dos *doss*	12	doce *dosseh*
3	tres *tress*	13	trece *tresseh*
4	cuatro *kwatro*	14	catorce *katorsseh*
5	cinco *seenko*	15	quince *keensseh*
6	seis *sayss*	16	dieciséis *dyessee-sayss*
7	siete *see-eh-teh*	17	diecisiete *dyessee-see-eh-teh*
8	ocho *otcho*	18	dieciocho *dyessee-otcho*
9	nueve *nweh-veh*	19	diecinueve *dyessee-nweh-veh*

20	veinte *vaynteh*
21	veintiuno *vayntee-oono*
22	veintidós *vayntee-doss*
30	treinta *traynta*
31	treinta y uno *trayntı oono*
32	treinta y dos *trayntı doss*
40	cuarenta *kwarenta*
50	cincuenta *seen-kwenta*
60	sesenta *sessenta*
70	setenta *setenta*
80	ochenta *otchenta*
90	noventa *no-venta*
100	cien *syen*
110	ciento diez *syento dyess*
200	doscientos, doscientas *doss-yentoss, doss-yentass*
500	quinientos, quinientas *keen-yentoss, keen-yentass*
700	setecientos, setecientas *seh-teh-syentoss, seh-teh-syentass*
1,000	mil *meel*
1,000,000	un millón *mee-yon*

* When **uno** precedes a masculine noun, it loses the final **o**, eg '1 point' is **un punto**. Feminine nouns take **una**, eg '1 peseta' **una peseta**. With numbers in the hundreds, 200, 300, 400 etc, the form ending in **-as** is used with feminine nouns, eg '300 notes' **trescientos billetes**; '300 pesetas' **trescientas pesetas**.

TIME, THE CALENDAR

today	hoy	*oy*
yesterday	ayer	*a-yair*
tomorrow	mañana	*man-yana*
the day before yesterday	anteayer	*anteh-a-yair*
the day after tomorrow	pasado mañana	*passado man-yana*
this week	esta semana	*esta semana*
last week	la semana pasada	*la semana passada*
next week	la semana que viene, la semana entrante	*la semana keh vyeh-neh, la semana entranteh*
this morning	esta mañana	*esta man-yana*
this afternoon	esta tarde	*esta tardeh*
this evening		
(up to 7pm)	esta tarde	*esta tardeh*
(from 7pm)	esta noche	*esta notcheh*
tonight	esta noche	*esta notcheh*
yesterday afternoon	ayer por la tarde	*a-yair por la tardeh*
last night	anoche	*anotcheh*
tomorrow morning	mañana por la mañana	*man-yana por la man-ya-na*
tomorrow night	mañana por la noche	*man-yana por la notcheh*
in three days	dentro de tres días	*dentro deh tress dee-ass*
three days ago	hace tres días	*a-seh tress dee-ass*
late	tarde	*tardeh*
early	pronto	*pronto*
soon	dentro de poco	*dentro deh poko*
later on	más tarde	*mass tardeh*
at the moment	en este momento	*en esteh momento*
second	un segundo	*segoondo*
minute	un minuto	*meenooto*
two minutes	dos minutos	*doss meenootoss*

quarter of an hour	un cuarto de hora	*kwarto deh ora*
half an hour	media hora	*mehd-ya ora*
three quarters of an hour	tres cuartos de hora	*tress kwartoss deh ora*
hour	la hora	*ora*
day	el día	*dee-a*
that day	ese día	*esseh dee-a*
every day	cada día	*kada dee-a*
all day	todo el día	*todo el dee-a*
the next day	el día siguiente	*el dee-a seeg-yenteh*
week	la semana	*semana*
fortnight, 2 weeks	la quincena	*keensseh-na*
month	el mes	*mess*
year	el año	*an-yo*

TELLING THE TIME

The 24-hour clock is commonly used in Latin America both in the written form (as in timetables) and verbally (for example, at tourist information desks etc). However, you will still hear the 12-hour clock used in everyday life.

'O'clock' is not normally translated in Spanish unless it is for emphasis, when **en punto** would be used. For example: (**es) la una (en punto)** is '(it's) one o'clock', whilst the plural form of the verb is used for all other hours, for example: (**son) las cinco (en punto)** is '(it's) five o'clock'.

The word 'past' is translated by **y** 'and'. In order to express minutes past the hour, state the hour followed by **y** plus the number of minutes: so **las seis y diez** is 'ten past six'. The word 'to' is translated by **para** – i.e. 'there are … (minutes) to go before …'. So, for example, **veinte para las diez** means 'twenty to ten'. The word for 'quarter' is **cuarto**; so, **un cuarto para las siete** is 'quarter to seven' and **las cinco y cuarto** is 'quarter past five'. 'Half past' is expressed using **y media**, so **las seis y media** is 'half past six'.

The word 'at' is translated by **a** followed by **las**; for example, **a las tres y cuarto** is 'at quarter past three'. Remember, however, to change **las** to **la** when using 'one', thus 'at half past one' is **a la una y media**.

The expressions 'am' and 'pm' have no direct equivalents but **de la mañana** 'in the morning', **de la tarde** 'in the afternoon/evening' (which extends up to about 7pm in Latin America) and **de la noche** 'at night' (from 7pm) are used to distinguish between times which might be confusing. For example, '6am' is **las seis de la mañana** and '6pm' is **las seis de la tarde**; '10am' is **las diez de la mañana** and '10pm' is **las diez de la noche**.

what time is it?	¿qué hora es?,	*keh ora ess,*
	¿qué horas son?	*keh orass son*
one o'clock	la una	*la oona*
ten past one	la una y diez	*la oona ee dyess*
quarter past one	la una y cuarto	*la oona ee kwarto*
twenty past one	la una y veinte	*la oona ee vaynteh*
half past one	la una y media	*la oona ee mehd-ya*
twenty to two	veinte para las dos	*vaynteh para lass doss*
quarter to two	un cuarto para las dos	*kwarto para lass doss*
two o'clock	las dos (en punto)	*lass doss (en poonto)*
13.00	las trece horas	*lass treh-seh orass*
16.30	las dieciséis treinta	*lass dyessee-sayss traynta*
20.10	las veinte diez	*lass vaynteh dyess*
noon	mediodía	*mehd-yo dee-a*
midnight	medianoche	*mehd-ya notcheh*

THE CALENDAR

The cardinal numbers on page 19 are used to express the date in Spanish. However, sometimes the ordinal number may be used instead, but only when used to express 'the first':

the first of May	el uno/el primero de mayo	*el oono/el preemehroh deh ma-yo*
the twentieth of June	el veinte de junio	*el vaynteh deh Hoon-yo*

HOTELS

There is an enormous variety of hotels and places to stay in Latin America. At the top of the scale are hotels classified by star ratings – the highest rating being five stars. At the lower end there may be little to distinguish hotels and **pensiones** (boarding houses). Boarding houses may be called **pensión**, **residencia**, **posada**, **hospedaje**, **casa familiar** or **casa de huespedes**. **Hosterías** and **dormitorios** are fairly basic and more akin to hostels with beds in shared rooms. Conditions in the different establishments vary from country to country, and it is possible that a **pensión** may prove to be cleaner and of a higher standard than a cheap hotel.

There are throughout Latin America hotels where couples can rent rooms for an hour or two. Obviously, these are not appropriate for someone seeking a place to stay. Such establishments are often motels and might be called **motel**, **hotel garaje** (Mex) or **albergue transitorio** (Arg), but the visitor should check if in doubt.

It's best to check out the room before committing yourself. It is also a good idea to find out whether rooms have individual showers, and whether they have constant or only intermittent hot water. In cheaper hotels, showers may be operated by an electric switch on the shower itself; these are often not earthed and therefore can be dangerous. It's not advisable to use the shaver socket in a bathroom for the same reason. Voltage varies from country to country.

USEFUL WORDS AND PHRASES

air-conditioned	con clima artificial	_kon kleema artee-feess-yal_
air-conditioner	el aire acondicionado	_ireh akondiss-yonado_
balcony	el balcón	_balkon_
bathroom	el (cuarto de) baño	_kwarto deh ban-yo_
bathtub	la bañera, la tina	_ban-yaira, teena_
bed	la cama	_kama_

23

bed and breakfast	cuarto con desayuno	*kwarto kon dessa-yoono*
bill	la cuenta	*kwenta*
boarding house	la pensión, la casa familiar	*penss-yon, la kassa famil-yar*
breakfast	el desayuno	*dessa-yoono*
dining room	el comedor	*komeh-dor*
dinner	la cena	*seh-na*
double bed	la cama doble, la cama matrimonial	*kama dobleh, kama matreemon-yal*
double room	un cuarto doble	*kwarto dobleh*
foyer	la entrada	*ent-rada*
full board	pensión completa	*penss-yon kompleh-ta*
half board	media pensión	*mehd-ya penss-yon*
hotel	el hotel	*otel*
key	la llave	*yaveh*
lift	el ascensor, el elevador	*ass-sensor, elevador*
lounge	la sala	*sala*
lunch	la comida, el almuerzo	*komeeda, almwairso*
manager	el/la gerente	*Hairenteh*
receipt	el recibo	*reh-seebo*
reception	la recepción	*reh-seps-yon*
receptionist	el/la recepcionista	*reh-seps-yoneesta*
room	la habitación, el cuarto, la pieza	*abeetass-yon, kwarto, pyeh-sa*
room service	el servicio de cuarto	*sairveess-yo deh kwarto*
shower	la ducha, la regadera (*Mex*)	*dootcha, reh-gadaira*
single bed	la cama individual	*kama eendeeveed-wal*
single room	un cuarto sencillo	*kwarto sensee-yo*
toilet (*room*)	los servicios, el baño (*Mex*)	*sairveess-yoss, ban-yo*
(*bowl*)	el retrete	*retreh-teh*

twin room	un cuarto con dos camas	*kwarto kon doss kamass*
washbasin	el lavamanos, el lavabo	*lavamanoss, lavabo*

Do you have any vacancies?
¿Tiene cuartos libres?
tyeh-neh kwartoss leebress

I have a reservation
Tengo reservación
tengo reh-sairvass-yon

I'd like a single room
Quisiera un cuarto sencillo
keess-yaira oon kwarto sensee-yo

I'd like a room with a balcony/bathroom
Quisiera un cuarto con balcón/baño
keess-yaira oon kwarto kon balkon/ban-yo

I'd like a room for one night/three nights
Quisiera un cuarto para una noche/para tres noches
keess-yaira oon kwarto para oona notcheh/para tress notchess

Can I see the room?
¿Me permite ver el cuarto?
meh pairmeeteh vair el kwarto

Do you have hot water all the time?
¿Hay agua caliente constante?
I agwa kal-yenteh konstanteh

What is the charge per night?
¿Cuánto cobra por noche?
kwanto kobra por notcheh

I don't know yet how long I'll stay
Todavía no sé cuánto tiempo me voy a quedar
todavee-a no seh kwanto tyempo meh voy a keh-dar

When is breakfast/dinner?
¿A qué hora es el desayuno/la cena?
a keh ora ess el dessa-yoono/la seh-na

Please wake me at 7 o'clock
Me puede llamar a las siete, por favor
meh pweh-deh yamar a lass syeh-teh por fa-vor

Can I have breakfast in my room?
¿Pueden servirme el desayuno en mi cuarto?
pweh-den sairveermeh el dessa-yoono en mee kwarto

I'd like to have some laundry done
Quisiera utilizar el servicio de lavado
keess-yaira ooteeleessar el sairveess-yo deh lavado

I'll be back at 10 o'clock
Regreso a las diez
reh-gresso a lass dyess

My room number is 205
El número de mi cuarto es el doscientos cinco
el noomairo deh mee kwarto ess el doss-yentoss seenko

I need a light bulb
Necesito una bombilla/un foco (Mex)/una lamparita (Arg)/
 un bombillo (Col)
*nessesseeto oona bombee-ya/oon foko/oona lampareeta/
 oon bombee-yo*

There is no toilet paper in the bathroom
Falta papel higiénico en el cuarto de baño
falta papel ee-Hygneeko en el kwarto deh ban-yo

The window won't open
La ventana no abre
la ventana no seh abreh

There isn't any hot water
No hay agua caliente
no I agwa kal-yenteh

I'm leaving tomorrow
Me voy mañana
meh voy man-yana

When do I have to vacate the room?
¿A qué hora debo desocupar?
a keh ora deh-bo dessokoopar

Can I have the bill, please?
¿Me da la cuenta, por favor?
meh da la kwenta por fa-vor

I'll pay by credit card
Quiero pagar con tarjeta (de crédito)
kyairo pagar kon tar-Heh-ta deh kredeeto

I'll pay cash
Voy a pagar en efectivo
voy a pagar en efekteevo

Can you get me a taxi?
¿Puede llamarme un taxi?
pwveh-deh yamarmeh oon taksee

Can you recommend another hotel?
¿Puede recomendarme otro hotel?
pweh-deh rekomendarmeh otro otel

THINGS YOU'LL SEE

acceso prohibido	staff only
alberca	swimming pool
albergue transitorio	motel
almuerzo	lunch
alojamiento	accommodation
ascensor	lift
baño	bathroom
cama con desayuno	bed and breakfast

→

casa de huespuedes	boarding house
casa familiar	boarding house
cena	dinner
comedor	dining room
comida	lunch, meal
completo	no vacancies
cuarto con dos camas	twin room
cuarto de baño	bathroom
cuarto doble	double room
cuarto individual	single room
cuarto matrimonial	double room
cuarto sencillo	single room
cuenta	bill
desayuno	breakfast
descuento	discount
dormitorio	hostel
ducha	shower
empujar	push
entrada	entrance
escaleras	stairs
hospedaje	boarding house
hostería	hostel
hotel garaje	motel
jalar	pull
media pensión	half board
pensión	boarding house
pensión completa	full board
piscina	swimming pool
posada	boarding house
primer piso	ground floor
prohibida la entrada	no admission
prohibido el paso	no entry
regadera	shower
residencia	boarding house
sala	lounge
salida de emergencia	emergency exit

→

segundo piso	first floor
servicio	service charge
servicios	toilet
sólo para residentes	hotel patrons only
tocador	ladies' room

THINGS YOU'LL HEAR

A la orden?
Can I help you?

Lo siento, está lleno
I'm sorry, we're full

El hotel está completo
We have no vacancies

No nos quedan habitaciones individuales/dobles
There are no single/double rooms left

¿Para cuántas noches?
For how many nights?

¿Va a pagar al contado o con tarjeta?
Will you be paying by cash or credit card?

Haga el favor de pagar por adelantado
Please pay in advance

Hay que desocupar antes de las doce
You must vacate the room by midday

CAMPING AND CARAVANNING

Camping is not as popular or as well organised as it is in much of Europe and North America and there are very few official campsites in Latin America. Cheap accommodation is generally available everywhere and camping can be a risky enterprise. It is not advisable to camp anywhere other than on an official site. In Argentina, Uruguay, Chile, Mexico and Guatemala camping holidays are becoming more popular and official sites are opening up. Youth hostels, called **albergues** or **hosterías** (the names vary according to country), are also available – you can obtain details from the **oficina de turismo** (tourist office) or the International Youth Hostelling Federation (IYHF).

USEFUL WORDS AND PHRASES

blanket	la cobija, la manta, la frazada (Mex, Chi, CAm)	kob<u>ee</u>-нa, m<u>a</u>nta, frass<u>a</u>da
bucket	el cubo, el balde	k<u>oo</u>bo, b<u>a</u>ldeh
Calor gas®	el cartucho de gas	kart<u>oo</u>tcho deh gass
campfire	una fogata	fog<u>a</u>ta
go camping	acampar	akamp<u>a</u>r
campsite	un camping	k<u>a</u>mpeen
caravan	la caravana, el tráiler	karav<u>a</u>na, tr<u>i</u>-ler
caravan site	un camping	k<u>a</u>mpeen
cooking utensils	los utensilios de cocina	ootens<u>ee</u>l-yoss deh koss<u>ee</u>na
drinking water	agua potable	<u>a</u>gwa pot<u>a</u>bleh
ground sheet	la lona impermeable	l<u>o</u>na eempairmeh-<u>a</u>bleh
hitchhike	hacer auto-stop, pedir cola, pedir ráid (CAm), pedir aventón (Mex)	ass<u>ai</u>r owtost<u>o</u>p, peh-d<u>ee</u>r kola, peh-d<u>ee</u>r r<u>i</u>d, peh-d<u>ee</u>r avent<u>o</u>n
rope	una cuerda	kw<u>ai</u>rda
rubbish	la basura	bass<u>oo</u>ra
saucepans	las cacerolas, las ollas (Mex)	kassairol<u>a</u>ss, <u>oy</u>-ass

sleeping bag	el saco de dormir	*sako deh dormeer*
tent	la carpa, la tienda de campaña *(Mex)*	*karpa, tyenda deh kampan-ya*
youth hostel	el albergue, la hostería	*albairgeh, ostairee-a*

Can I camp here?
¿Puedo acampar aquí?
pweh-do akampar akee

Can we park the caravan here?
¿Podemos estacionar aquí el tráiler?
podeh-moss estass-yonar akee el trı-ler

Where is the nearest campsite?
¿Dónde está el camping más cercano?
dondeh esta el kampeen mass sairkano

What is the charge per night?
¿Cuánto cobra por noche?
kwanto kobra por notcheh

How much is it for a week?
¿Cuánto es para una semana?
kwanto ess para oona semana

I only want to stay for one night
Es para una noche sólo
ess para oona notcheh solo

Where is the kitchen?
¿Dónde está la cocina?
dondeh esta la kosseena

Can I light a fire here?
¿Puedo hacer fuego aquí?
pweh-do assair fweh-go akee

Where can I get …?
¿Dónde consigo …?
dondeh konseego

Is there any drinking water?
¿Hay agua potable?
I _agwa potableh_

THINGS YOU'LL SEE

agua	water
agua potable	drinking water
albergue juvenil	youth hostel
aseos	toilet and washroom
baños	toilet and washroom
camping	campsite
cocina	kitchen, cooker, stove
duchas	showers
estufa	cooker, stove
hostería	youth hostel
linterna	torch
no bañarse	no swimming
no se admiten perros	no dogs allowed
oficina de turismo	tourist office
para uso de ...	for the use of ...
precio	price
prohibido ...	no ...
prohibido acampar	no camping
prohibido el paso	no trespassing
prohibido prender fuego	no campfires
regadera	shower
se alquila	for hire
se alquilan sacos de dormir	sleeping bags for hire
se arrienda	for hire
se prohíbe ...	... forbidden
tarifa	charges
tienda	shop

DRIVING

There is a wide variation in the quality and type of roads the motorist will find in Latin America. Major inter-city motorways (**autopistas**) are usually of a reasonable standard, although they will often be toll-roads (**autopista de peaje**) and can be expensive. There will usually be an older and poorer road without tolls. Secondary roads, by contrast, can vary greatly and in some cases will be little more than dirt tracks (**caminos de tierra**).

Travelling across borders by car will often involve several bureaucratic procedures. Motorists should always carry registration documents and an international driving licence. Insurance requirements vary, but foreigners are usually required to take out insurance, although many local drivers won't be insured. It is normal for customs to stamp your passport or provide documentation of some kind – without this it may prove difficult to leave the country. In case of an accident, it is likely that the motorist will be required to make an instant payment irrespective of who is at fault; but it might be possible to recover this later through one's insurance.

The variety of terrain makes it advisable to use sturdy and if possible four-wheel drive vehicles for any journey that is likely to involve straying from the beaten track. Unleaded petrol is hard to find outside Mexico, but diesel is generally available. Petrol is dirtier than it is in Britain or the United States, so spark plugs etc should be more regularly checked.

Every village has its resident mechanic; in general they are very skilled, but the visitor should check prices before the work is done.

The foreign motorist is always vulnerable to theft of the car or its parts. It is as well not to leave the car unattended, not to leave anything in view that might encourage theft, and perhaps, if all else fails, to accept the offer from the inevitable crowd of small boys to 'look after your car' in exchange for money.

It is a common occurrence in Latin America to be stopped at a road block on the motorway or in a city. Visitors should carry all their documents with them and be ready to show them. If that is not enough, and the person who has stopped you seems intent on finding some offence to charge you with, it may be money that they want – and you may have to negotiate an 'instant fine'.

The rules of the road are: drive on the right, overtake on the left. In the case of roads having equal status, or at unmarked junctions, traffic coming from the right has priority. In general, however, it is wise to assume that the rules will be ignored as often as not. Speed limits vary from country to country.

Fuel ratings are as follows: **normal**: 2-star; **super**: 3-star; **extra**: 4-star; **gas-oil**: diesel; **sin plomo**: unleaded.

Parking is often restricted in urban areas, and cars will rapidly be clamped and removed. Try to park in an official car park.

SOME COMMON ROAD SIGNS

aduana	customs
alto	stop
apagar luces	headlights off
atención al tren	beware of trains
autopista	motorway
autopista de peaje	toll road
callejón sin salida	dead end
calle peatonal	pedestrian precinct
calzada deteriorada	bad surface
calzada irregular	uneven surface
cambio de sentido	junction
carretera cortada	road closed
ceda el paso	give way
centro ciudad	town centre
centro urbano	town centre
cerrado por obras	road closed for repairs
circulación	traffic; traffic direction
circule despacio	slow
circunvalación	ring road
cruce	crossroads

→

desviación	detour
desvío	detour
desvío provisional	temporary detour
escuela	school
estacionamiento	car park
final de autopista	end of motorway
firme en mal estado	bad surface
hielo	ice
información turística	tourist information
no corretear	no overtaking
no hay arcén	no hard shoulder
no rebasar	no overtaking
obras	roadworks
¡ojo!	danger!
ojo al tren	beware of trains
paso a desnivel	underpass
paso a nivel	level crossing
paso subterráneo	underpass
peaje	toll
peatón, circule por la izquierda	pedestrians, keep to the left
peatones	pedestrians
peligro	danger
peligro deslizamientos	slippery road surface
precaución	caution
prender luces de cruce	headlights on
prohibido el paso	no trespassing
prohibido estacionarse	no parking
puesto de socorro	first aid
salida de camiones	works exit
se usa grúa	cars will be towed away
vado permanente	in constant use (no parking)
vehículos pesados	heavy vehicles
velocidad controlada por radar	radar speed check
zona de estacionamento limitado	restricted parking zone

USEFUL WORDS AND PHRASES

bonnet	el capó, el capote, el cofre (Mex)	*kapo, kapoteh, kofreh*
boot	el maletero, la maleta, el baúl (Per), la cajuela (Mex)	*maleh-tairo, maleh-ta, ba-ool, kaнweh-la*
brake	el freno	*freh-no*
breakdown	una descompostura, una pana	*desskompostoora, pana*
car	el auto, el automóvil, el carro (Mex)	*owto, owtomoveel, karro*
caravan	la caravana, el tráiler	*karavana, trı-lair*
car park	el estacionamiento	*estass-yonam-yento*
clutch	el embrague	*embrageh*
crossroads	el cruce	*kroosseh*
drive	manejar	*maneh-нar*
driving licence	el carnet de conducir, el permiso de conducir, el brevete (Per, Col)	*karneh deh kondoosseer, pairmeesso deh kondoosseer, breveh-teh*
engine	el motor	*motor*
exhaust	el tubo de escape, el exosto (Arg)	*toobo deh eskapeh, ekss-osto*
fanbelt	la correa del ventilador	*korreh-a del venteelador*
garage (*repairs*) (*for petrol*)	el taller, el garaje la gasolinera, el grifo (Per)	*ta-yair, gara-нeh gassoleenaira, greefo*
gear	el cambio	*kamb-yo*
gear box	la caja de velocidades	*ka-нa deh velosseedadess*
gears	los cambios	*kamb-yoss*
headlights	las luces de cruce	*loossess deh kroosseh*
hose (*pipe*)	la manguera	*mangaira*

indicator *(light)*	el intermitente	*eentairmeetenteh*
jack	el gato	*gato*
junction	el entronque	*entronkeh*
(motorway entry)	una entrada de autopista	*entrada deh owtopeesta*
(motorway exit)	una salida de autopista	*saleeda deh owtopeesta*
mirror	el (espejo) retrovisor	*espeh-Ho retroveessor*
motorbike	la moto (cicleta)	*motosseekleh-ta*
motorway	la autopista	*owtopeesta*
number plate	la matrícula, la placa *(Mex)*, la chapa *(Arg)*	*matreekoola, plaka, chapa*
petrol	la gasolina, la nafta *(Arg)*, la bencina *(Chi)*	*gassoleena, nafta, benseena*
petrol station	una gasolinera, un grifo *(Per)*	*gassoleenaira, greefo*
rear lights	las luces piloto, las calaveras *(Mex)*	*loossess peeloto, kalavairass*
road *(street)*	la calle	*ka-yeh*
(main road)	la carretera	*karrehtaira*
spares	los repuestos, las refacciones *(Mex)*	*reh-pwestoss, rehfaks-yoness*
spark plug	la bujía	*boo-Hee-a*
speed	la velocidad	*velosseeda*
speed limit	el límite de velocidad	*leemeeteh deh velosseeda*
speedometer	el cuentakilómetros	*kwenta-keelomeh-tross*
steering wheel	el volante, el timón *(Arg)*	*volanteh, teemon*
tow	remolcar	*reh-molkar*
traffic lights	el semáforo	*seh-maforo*
trailer	el remolque	*reh-molkeh*
truck	el camión	*kam-yon*

tyre	la llanta,	*yanta,*
	la goma *(Arg, Uru)*,	*goma,*
	el caucho *(Ven)*	*kowcho*
tyre lever	el calzo para	*kalsso para*
	rueda	*rweda*
van	la camioneta	*kam-yoneta*
wheel	la rueda	*rweh-da*
windscreen	el parabrisas	*parabreessass*
windscreen	el limpiaparabrisas	*leemp-ya*
wiper		*parabreessass*

I'd like some petrol/oil/water
Quisiera gasolina/aceite/agua
keess-yaira gassoleena/assay-teh/agwa

Fill her up, please!
¡Lleno, por favor!
yeh-no por fa-vor

35 litres of 4-star (premium), please
Póngame treinta y cinco litros de extra
pongameh traynti seenko leetross deh extra

Would you check the tyres, please?
¿Me revisa las llantas, por favor?
meh reveessa lass yantass por fa-vor

Do you do repairs?
¿Hacen reparaciones?
a-ssen reparass-yoness

Can you repair the clutch?
¿Pueden arreglarme el embrague?
pweh-den arreh-glarmeh el embrageh

How long will it take?
¿Cuánto tardarán?
kwanto tardaran

There is something wrong with the engine
Hay algo que marcha mal en el motor
I algo keh marcha mal en el motor

The engine is overheating
El motor se calienta demasiado
el motor seh kal-yenta demass-yado

I need a new tyre
Necesito llanta nueva
nessesseeto yanta nweh-va

I'd like to rent a car
Quisiera alquilar un auto/un carro (Mex)
keess-yaira alkeelar oon owto/oon karro

I'd like an automatic/a manual
Quisiera un auto/un carro (Mex) automático/manual
keess-yaira oon owto/oon karro owtomateeko/manwal

Is there a mileage charge?
¿Tiene suplemento por kilómetro?
tyeh-neh sooplemento por keelometro

Where is the nearest garage? (for repairs)
¿Dónde está el taller más cercano?
dondeh esta el ta-yair mass sairkano

Where is the nearest petrol station?
¿Dónde está la gasolinera más cercana/el grifo (Per) más cercano?
dondeh esta la gassoleenaira mass sairkana/el greefo mass sairkano

Where can I park?
¿Dónde puedo estacionarme?
dondeh pweh-do estass-yonarmeh

Can I park here?
¿Puedo estacionarme aquí?
pweh-do estass-yonarmeh akee

How do I get to Lima?
¿Cómo se llega a Lima?
komo seh yeh-ga a leema

Is this the road to Monterrey?
¿Es éste el camino de Monterrey?
ess esteh el kameeno deh monteh-ray

DIRECTIONS YOU MAY BE GIVEN

a la derecha/izquierda	on the right/left
después de pasar el/la ...	after the ...
doble a la derecha	take a right
la primera a la derecha	first on the right
la segunda a la izquierda	second on the left
todo derecho	straight on
todo recto	straight on
voltee a la izquierda	take a left

THINGS YOU'LL SEE

aceite	oil
agua	water
aire	air
ángeles verdes	Mexican road assistance service
apague el motor	switch off engine
composturas	repairs
entrada	entrance, way in
estacionamiento subterráneo	underground car park
estación de servicio	service station
extra	4-star
garaje	garage

→

gas-oil	diesel
gasolina	petrol
gasolinera	filling station
haga cola aquí	queue/wait here
introduzca el dinero exacto	insert exact change
lleno	full
magna sin	unleaded petrol
nivel del aceite	oil level
normal	2-star
nova	leaded petrol
presión	air pressure
presión de las llantas	tyre pressure
prohibido fumar	no smoking
recoja su ticket	take a ticket
reparación	repairs
salida	exit, way out
sin plomo	unleaded
solo para residentes del hotel	hotel patrons only
super	3-star
taller (de reparaciones)	garage
(tren de) lavado automático	car wash
zona de servicios	service area

Things You'll Hear

¿Lo quiere automático o manual?
Would you like an automatic or a manual?

Su carnet de conducir/permiso de conducir/licencia, por favor
May I see your driving licence, please?

Su carnet de chofer/licencia/brevete, por favor
May I see your driving licence, please?

Su pasaporte, por favor
Your passport, please

Usted ha cometido una infracción
You have committed an offence

TRAVELLING AROUND

AIR TRAVEL

Numerous international airlines provide services to the major cities of Latin America. Most Latin American countries have at least one national airline; many state airlines are currently being privatised or fused with existing private companies. Internal air travel within countries is also quite common and not necessarily expensive, since road and rail access is not available to a number of areas – the cities of the Amazon region, for example.

RAIL TRAVEL

Generally speaking, Latin American trains are cheap, though of varying degrees of comfort. Take note that the slow local trains are sometimes misleadingly called **expresos** or **rápidos**. Most trains are slow when compared to long-distance buses, even between major cities. The main types of train are:

ferrobús	fast intercity train
autovagón	fast intercity train (*Per*)
servicio estrella	luxury intercity train (*Mex*)
rápido	moderately fast train, first class train (*Chi*)
expreso	slow train stopping at all stations, fast train (*Bol*)
tren de lujo	first class train
tren de pasajeros	passenger train
tren local	local train
tren mixto	mixed freight/passenger train

On some trains you may also have the option of a fixed seat (**asiento fijo**) or an adjustable/reclining seat (**asiento reclinable**).

LONG-DISTANCE BUS TRAVEL

Buses remain the most popular form of travel. The range of
services is wide, from the luxury air-conditioned coach
(**pullman**) to the cheaper, less comfortable service (**ordinario**
or **de segunda clase**). It is almost always necessary to book
seats on long-distance buses and the quality of vehicles varies
greatly from country to country.

LOCAL TRANSPORT

Local buses also vary from country to country, but they
generally have a flat fare wherever you are going, show their
destination on the front, and are invariably crowded. The
larger, more modern buses may cost fractionally more. You can
also travel in minibuses or large vans (usually called **micro** or
combi) as well as, in some places, trucks or lorries with
wooden seats.

  Mexico City, Santiago, Caracas and Buenos Aires all have
underground/subway (**metro, subte** (*Arg*)) systems. They also
have a flat-fare system.

TAXI AND BOAT, OTHER TRANSPORT

In most Latin American cities there are collective taxis
(**colectivo/pesero**) which carry a number of passengers for a
fixed fare on a fixed route. These will often be minibuses or
large cars with distinctive markings. There are also individual
taxis which can be hailed in the street if they show the 'for
hire' sign (**libre**). It is always wise to agree a price before you
get in, since drivers will frequently not use taxi meters.
Airports and hotels often have taxis which are more expensive
and usually more luxurious.

  In several countries water transport is common, usually in
the form of a ferry boat (**transbordadora**) or a smaller powered
boat (**lancha**).

Useful Words and Phrases

adult	un adulto	*ad__oo__lto*
adults	mayores	*ma-y__o__ress*
air-conditioned	con aire acondicionado	*kon __ī__reh akondiss-yon__a__do*
airport	el aeropuerto	*a-airopw__ai__rto*
airport bus	el autobús del aeropuerto	*owtob__oo__ss del a-airopw__ai__rto*
airport tax	la tasa aeroportuaria	*t__a__ssa a-airoportw__a__r-ya*
aisle seat	un asiento de pasillo	*ass-y__e__nto deh pass__ee__-yo*
baggage	el equipaje	*ekeep__a__-Heh*
baggage claim	la recogida de equipajes	*reko-H__ee__da deh ekeep__a__-Hess*
boarding card	la tarjeta de embarque	*tar-H__e__h-ta deh emb__a__rkeh*
boat	el barco, la lancha	*b__a__rko, l__a__ntcha*
buffet	la cafetería	*kafeh-tair__ee__-a*
bus	el autobús	*owtob__oo__ss*
(long-distance)	el ómnibus, la góndola (*Chi*)	*__o__mneeb__oo__ss, g__o__ndola*
(local)	el camión (*Mex*), la camioneta (*Gua*), el guagua (*Cub*), la micro (*Chi*), la buseta (*Col, Ecu*)	*kam-y__o__n, kam-yon__e__h-ta, w__a__-wa, m__ee__kro, booss__e__h-ta*
bus station	la terminal de autobuses, la central de autobuses	*tairmeen__a__l deh owtob__oo__ssess, sentr__a__l deh owtob__oo__ssess*
bus stop	la parada del autobús	*par__a__da del owtob__oo__ss*
carriage	el vagón, el coche	*vag__o__n, k__o__tcheh*
check-in desk	la mesa de facturación	*m__e__h-sa deh faktoorass-y__o__n*

child	un niño/una niña	neen-yo/neen-ya
compartment	el compartimento	komparteemento
connection	una correspondencia	koreh-spondenss-ya
cruise	un crucero	kroossairo
customs	la aduana	adwana
departure lounge	la sala de pasajeros	sala deh passa-Haiross
domestic	nacional	nass-yonal
driver	el chofer	chofer
emergency exit	la salida de emergencia	saleeda deh eh-mairHenss-ya
entrance	la entrada	entrada
exit	la salida	saleeda
ferry	la transbordadora	transborda-dora
first class	primera (clase)	preemaira klasseh
fixed seat	un asiento fijo	ass-yento fee-Ho
flight	el vuelo	vweh-lo
flight number	el número de vuelo	noomairo deh vweh-lo
foreign exchange	el cambio de moneda	kamb-yo deh moneh-da
gate	la puerta (de embarque)	pwairta deh embarkeh
hand luggage	el equipaje de mano	ekeepa-Heh deh mano
international	internacional	eentairnass-yonal
left-luggage office	la consigna	konseegna
lost property office	la oficina de objetos perdidos	ofeesseena deh obHeh-toss pairdeedoss
luggage	el equipaje	ekeepa-Heh
luggage trolley	un carrito para el equipaje	karreeto para el ekeepa-Heh
network map	un plano	plano
non-smoking	no fumadores	no foomadoress
number 5 bus	el (autobús número) cinco	owtobooss noomairo seenko
one-way ticket	un boleto de ida, un pasaje de ida	boleh-to deh eeda, passa-Heh deh eeda

passport	el pasaporte	*passaporteh*
platform	la vía/plataforma	*vee-a/plataforma*
port	el puerto	*pwairto*
quay	el muelle	*mweh-yeh*
railway	el ferrocarril	*ferro-karreel*
reclining seat	un asiento reclinable	*ass-yento rekleenableh*
reserved seat	un asiento reservado	*ass-yento reh-sairvado*
restaurant car	el coche-comedor	*kotcheh komeh-dor*
return ticket	un boleto de ida y vuelta, un pasaje de ida y vuelta	*boleh-to deh eeda ee vwelta, passa-Heh deh eeda ee vwelta*
schedule	el horario	*orar-yo*
seat	un asiento	*ass-yento*
second class	segunda (clase)	*segoonda klasseh*
single ticket	un boleto de ida, un pasaje de ida	*boleh-to deh eeda, passa-Heh deh eeda*
sleeping car	el coche-dormitorio	*kotcheh dormeetoree-o*
smoking	fumadores	*foomadoress*
station	la estación	*estass-yon*
subway (*walkway*)	paso subterráneo	*passo soobterraneh-o*
subway (*transport*)	el metro, el subte (*Arg*)	*meh-tro, soobteh*
taxi	un taxi	*taksee*
(*collective*)	un colectivo, un pesero	*kolekteevo, pessairo*
terminus (*bus*)	la terminal	*tairmeenal*
(*rail*)	la estación terminal	*estass-yon tairmeenal*
ticket	un boleto, un pasaje	*boleh-to, passa-Heh*
ticket office	la oficina de boletos	*ofeesseena deh boleh-toss*
timetable	el horario	*orar-yo*
train	el tren	*tren*

underground	el metro,	*meh-tro,*
	el subte *(Arg)*	*soobteh*
waiting room	la sala de espera	*sala deh espaira*
window seat	un asiento de	*ass-yento deh*
	ventanilla	*ventanee-ya*

AIR TRAVEL

A non-smoking seat, please
Un asiento en la sección de no fumadores, por favor
oon ass-yento en la sekss-yon deh no fooma-doress por fa-vor

I'd like a window seat, please
Quisiera un asiento junto a la ventanilla, por favor
keess-yaira oon ass-yento Hoonto a la ventanee-ya por fa-vor

How long will the flight be delayed?
¿Cuánto tiempo va a demorar el vuelo?
kwanto tyempo va a demorar el vweh-lo

Which gate for the flight to Mexico City?
¿Cuál es la puerta de embarque para el vuelo de México?
kwal ess la pwairta deh embarkeh para el vweh-lo deh meh-Hee-ko

RAIL, BUS AND UNDERGROUND TRAVEL

When does the train/bus for Santiago leave?
¿A qué hora sale el tren/autobús para Santiago?
a keh ora saleh el tren/owtobooss para santee-ago

When does the train/bus from Guadalajara arrive?
¿A qué hora llega el tren/autobús de Guadalajara?
a keh ora yeh-ga el tren/owto-booss deh gwadala-Hara

When is the next train/bus to Lima?
¿A qué hora sale el próximo tren/autobús para Lima?
a keh ora saleh el prokseemo tren/owtobooss para leema

When is the first/last train/bus to Bogota?
¿A qué hora sale el primer/último tren/autobús para Bogotá?
a keh ora saleh el preemair/oolteemo tren/owtobooss para bogota

How much is it to Buenos Aires?
¿Cuánto es el boleto para Buenos Aires?
kwanto ess el boleh-to para bweh-noss _i_-ress

Do I have to pay a supplement?
¿Hay que pagar suplemento?
_i_ keh pagar soopleh-mento

Do I have to change trains?
¿Tengo que hacer correspondencia?
tengo keh assair korrespondenss-ya

Does the train/bus stop at Rosario?
¿Se para el tren/autobús en Rosario?
seh para el tren/owto-booss en rossaree-o

How long does it take to get to Cordoba?
¿Cuánto se tarda en llegar a Córdoba?
kwanto seh tarda en yeh-gar a kordoba

Where can I buy a ticket?
¿Dónde puedo comprar boleto/pasaje?
dondeh pweh-do komprar boleh-to/passa-нeh

REPLIES YOU MAY BE GIVEN

El próximo tren sale a las dieciocho horas
The next train leaves at 1800 hours

Haga la correspondencia en Cuzco
Change at Cuzco

Tiene que pagar suplemento
You must pay a supplement

Ya no quedan asientos para Asunción
There are no more seats available for Asunción

49

A single (one-way) ticket to San Salvador, please
Un boleto/un pasaje de ida a San Salvador, por favor
oon boleh-to/oon passa-Heh deh eeda a san salvador por fa-vor

A return (round-trip) ticket to Cali, please
Un boleto/un pasaje de ida y vuelta a Cali, por favor
oon boleh-to/oon passa-Heh deh eeda ee vwelta a kalee por fa-vor

Could you help me get a ticket?
¿Podría usted ayudarme a sacar boleto/pasaje?
podree-a oosteh a-yoodarmeh a sakar boleh-to/passa-Heh

I'd like to reserve a seat
Quisiera reservar un asiento
keess-yaira reh-sairvar oon ass-yento

Is this the right train/bus for Quito?
¿Es éste el tren/autobús para Quito?
ess esteh el tren/owto-booss para keeto

Is this the right platform for the Monterrey train?
¿El tren de Monterrey sale de esta vía?
el tren deh monteh-ray saleh deh esta vee-a

Which platform for the Granada train?
¿Qué vía para el tren de Granada?
keh vee-a para el tren deh granada

Is the train/bus late?
¿Se demoró el tren/autobús?
seh deh-moro el tren/owtobooss

Could you help me with my baggage, please?
¿Me ayuda con estas maletas, por favor?
meh a-yooda kon estass maleh-tass por fa-vor

Is this a non-smoking compartment?
¿Está prohibido fumar aquí?
esta pro-eebeedo foomar akee

Is this seat free?
¿Está libre este asiento?
esta leebreh esteh ass-yento

This seat is taken
Este asiento está ocupado
esteh ass-yento esta okoopado

I have reserved this seat
Tengo reservado este asiento
tengo reh-sairvado esteh ass-yento

May I open/close the window?
¿Puedo abrir/cerrar la ventana?
pweh-do abreer/serrar la ventana

When do we arrive in Caracas?
¿A qué hora llegamos a Caracas?
a keh ora yeh-gamoss a karakass

What station is this?
¿Qué estación es ésta?
keh estass-yon ess esta

Do we stop at Cuzco?
¿Nos paramos en Cuzco?
noss paramoss en koossko

Would you keep an eye on my things for a moment?
¿Me vigila las cosas un momento?
meh veeнeela lass kossass oon momento

Is there a restaurant car on this train?
¿Tiene coche-comedor este tren?
tyeh-neh kotcheh komeh-dor esteh tren

Where is the nearest underground station?
¿Dónde está la estación de metro más cercana?
dondeh esta la estass-yon deh meh-tro mass sairkana

Where is there a bus stop?
¿Dónde hay una parada de bús?
dondeh I oona parada deh booss

Which buses go to Merida?
¿Qué autobuses van a Mérida?
keh owtoboossess van a maireeda

How often do the buses to Veracruz run?
¿Cada cuánto tiempo pasan los autobuses para Veracruz?
kada kwanto tyempo pasan loss owtoboossess para vairakrooss

Will you let me know when we're there?
¿Puede avisarme cuando lleguemos?
pweh-deh aveess-armeh kwando yeh-geh-moss

Do I have to get off yet?
¿Tengo que bajarme ya?
tengo keh ba-Harmeh ya

How do you get to Rosario?
¿Cómo se llega a Rosario?
komo seh yeh-ga a rossaree-o

Do you go near San Pedro?
¿Pasa usted cerca de San Pedro?
pasa oosteh sairka deh san peh-dro

Next stop, please!
¡Bajan!/¡Esquina!
ba-Han/eskeena

TAXI AND BOAT

Where can I get a taxi?
¿Dónde consigo un taxi?
dondeh konseego oon taksee

To the airport, please
Al aeropuerto, por favor
al a-airopwairto por fa-vor

Can you take me to the city centre?
¿Me lleva al centro?
meh yeh-va al sentro

Can you let me out here?
Me deja aquí, por favor
meh deh-ha akee por fa-vor

How much is it to the station?
¿Cuánto cuesta ir a la estación?
kwanto kwesta eer a la estass-yon

That's too much!
¡Es demasiado!
ess deh-mass-yado

Could you wait here for me and take me back?
¿Me espera aquí para llevarme de regreso?
meh espaira akee para yeh-varmeh deh reh-gresso

Where can I get the ferry to Colón?
¿Dónde tomo la transbordadora para Colón?
dondeh tomo la transborda-dora para kolon

THINGS YOU'LL SEE

aduana	customs
alcoba	berth
a los trenes	to the trains
asientos	seats
atraso	delay
autotren	motorail
autovagón	fast intercity train
boletos	tickets, ticket office
bus-cama	sleeper bus
camarín	sleeping compartment
cambio de moneda	foreign exchange

→

camión	bus
carnet	book of underground/ subway tickets
central camionera	bus station
central de autobuses	bus station
climatizado	air-conditioned
coche-dormitorio	sleeper, sleeping car
colectivo	minibus, taxi
combi	collective taxi
consigna	left-luggage office, baggage check
control de pasaportes	passport control
correspondencia	connection
demora	delay
domingos y feriados	Sundays and public holidays
entrada	entrance
entrada por delante/ por detrás	entry at the front/rear
equipajes	left-luggage office, baggage check
escala	intermediate stop
estación	station
estación principal	central station
estación terrestre	bus station
excepto domingos	Sundays excepted
expreso	slow train stopping at all stations, (Bol) fast train
facturación	check-in
ferrobús	intercity fast train
ficha(s)	tokens for underground/ subway
fumadores	smokers
hacer correspondencia en ...	change at ...
hora local	local time
horario	timetable, schedule
laborables	weekdays
libre	vacant; for hire

→

llegadas	arrivals
mayores	adults
menores	children
metro	underground, subway
multa por uso indebido	penalty for misuse
nacional	domestic
niños	children
no fumadores	non-smokers
no fumar	no smoking
no hay parada en ...	does not stop in ...
no para en ...	does not stop in ...
ocupado	engaged, occupied
pague el importe exacto	no change given
parada	stop
pasajes	tickets, ticket office
pesero	collective taxi
por puesto	minibus
prensa	newsstand
primera clase	first class
prohibida la entrada	no entry
prohibido asomarse a la ventana	do not lean out of the window
prohibido el paso	no entry
prohibido fumar	no smoking
prohibido hablar con el chofer	do not speak to the driver
puerta de embarque	gate
puerto	harbour
puesto de periódicos	newsstand
pullman	luxury bus
rápido	moderately fast train, (*Chi*) first class train
recogida de equipajes	baggage claim
reservación de asientos	seat reservation
ruta	route
sala de espera	waiting room

→

salida	departure; exit
salida de emergencia	emergency exit
salidas	departures
salón	first class
segunda clase	second class
servicio estrella	luxury intercity train/bus
sólo laborables	weekdays only
suplemento	supplement
taquilla	ticket office
terminal	terminus
terminal de autobuses	bus station
terminal terrestre	bus station
tiquetes	tickets
tren de lujo	first class train
tren de pasajeros	passenger train
tren local	local train
tren mixto	mixed freight/passenger train
trenes de cercanías	local trains
utilice sólo sencillo	small change only
vagón	carriage
vía	platform, track
viaje	journey
vuelo	flight
vuelo directo	direct flight
vuelo regular	scheduled flight

THINGS YOU'LL HEAR

¿Lleva equipaje?
Do you have any baggage?

¿Fumadores o no fumadores?
Smoking or non-smoking?

¿Asiento de ventanilla o de pasillo?
Window seat or aisle seat?

→

Está completo
It's full

Su boleto, por favor
Can I see your ticket, please?

Los pasajeros del vuelo tres dos cuatro, con destino a Londres, están en estos momentos embarcando en el avión
Passengers for flight 324 for London are requested to proceed to embarkation

Pasen a la puerta (número) cuatro
Please go now to gate (number) four

Los boletos, por favor
Tickets, please

Suban
Board (the train)

El tren con destino a Granada saldrá de la vía número seis dentro de diez minutos
The train for Granada will leave from platform six in ten minutes

El tren de Monterrey llegará a la vía número uno dentro de cinco minutos
The train from Monterrey will arrive at platform one in five minutes

El tren con destino a Corinto lleva quince minutos de retraso
The train for Corinto is running 15 minutes late

Sus boletos listos, por favor
Have your tickets ready, please

Abra sus maletas, por favor
Open your suitcases, please

RESTAURANTS

Restaurants (**restaurante**) vary greatly in quality and price, so
look at the menu (**la carta**) first. But if their name includes the
words **posada** or **mesón** they are probably more expensive.
Cheaper restaurants may carry other names, or indeed may not
have a name at all. In Mexico the cheap eating places are
called **cocina económica**; in Central America they are known
as **fritanga** and **pupusería** and in Costa Rica **soda** – but **café** is
the general word. In Peru and Chile, Chinese food is found
everywhere and is often cheap – **chifa** is the word for both
Chinese food and Chinese restaurants. **Pizzerías** are universal,
as are roast chicken restaurants (**rosticería** or **pollería**). There
are fast food chains everywhere, and the **hamburguesas** that
they sell will be immediately recognisable. Mexican food has
become international and is best known for the variety of filled
corn or wheat pancakes (**tortillas** and **tacos**) sold in **taquerías**.
Eating out in Cuba can be difficult because of the chronic
shortages affecting the economy; hotels will often have a
set-price buffet or **oferta especial**.

  If you are travelling on a tight budget it is best to look for set
menus, which are usually cheaper. The signs will say
almuerzo, **menú**, **comida típica**, **comida corriente** (*CAm*) or
comida corrida (*Mex*), but if there is no sign you should ask if
there is a set menu. The cheapest food is found in the markets,
but it is probably wise to wait until you are used to the food
before you eat there.

  Breakfast may be a light meal, but in Mexico, for example, a
hotel breakfast can be an enormous affair with fruit and eggs
and meat dishes. Lunch, eaten between 2 and 4pm, is usually
the heaviest meal and will often be followed by a siesta.
Certainly, lunch time will be a period when very little happens. The
evening meal, taken between 6 and 9pm will normally be lighter.

  Tea, coffee and cakes can be eaten in a **confitería** or **salón de
té**. Alcohol is sold in a **bar**, or a **cantina** (*Mex*). In Mexico,
there is also the **pulquería** where Mexicans drink flavoured
varieties of the thick white drink (**pulque**) distilled from the

agave cactus; in Peru, a **chichería** is the place where you can
buy local spirits. A **cervecería** (or a **choppería** in the south of
the continent) sells beer.

USEFUL WORDS AND PHRASES

beer	una cerveza,	*sairveh-sa,*
	un chop *(Chi)*	*chop*
bill	la cuenta	*kwenta*
bottle	la botella	*botay-ya*
bread	el pan	*pan*
butter	la mantequilla	*manteh-kee-ya*
café	una cafetería	*kaffeh-tairee-a*
cake	un pastel,	*pastel,*
	un queque,	*keh-keh,*
	una torta	*torta*
coffee	el café	*kaffeh*
(black)	un café solo,	*kaffeh solo,*
	un americano *(Mex)*,	*amaireekano,*
	un tinto *(Col)*	*teento*
(dash of milk)	un cortado	*kortado*
cup	la taza	*tassa*
fork	el tenedor	*teneh-dor*
glass *(tumbler)*	el vaso	*va-so*
(wine glass)	la copa	*kopa*
half-litre	medio litro	*mehd-yo leetro*
knife	el cuchillo	*kootchee-yo*
litre	litro	*leetro*
menu	la carta	*karta*
milk	la leche	*letcheh*
mineral water	el agua mineral	*agwa meenairal*
(still)	el agua mineral	*agwa meenairal*
	sin gas	*seen gass*
(fizzy)	el agua mineral	*agwa meenairal*
	con gas	*kon gass*
napkin	la servilleta	*sairvee-yeh-ta*
pepper	la pimienta	*peem-yenta*

plate	el plato	*plato*
receipt	un recibo	*resseebo*
restaurant	un restaurante	*restowranteh*
salt	la sal	*sal*
sandwich	un sandwich,	*sandweetch,*
	una torta (Mex)	*torta*
set menu	el menú, el almuerzo,	*menoo, almwairsso,*
	la comida típica,	*komeeda teepeeka,*
	la comida corriente	*komeeda korr-yenteh*
	(CAm),	
	la comida corrida (Mex)	*komeeda korreeda*
spoon	la cuchara	*kootchara*
sugar	el azúcar, el dulce	*assookar, doolseh*
(raw)	el piloncillo	*peelonsee-yo*
table	la mesa	*meh-sa*
tea	el té	*teh*
(bitter tea)	el mate (Arg)	*mateh*
teaspoon	la cucharilla	*kootcharee-ya*
waiter	el mozo,	*mo-so,*
	el mesero (Mex, CAm),	*messairo,*
	el garzón (Arg,	*garsson,*
	Uru, Chi),	
	el mesonero (Ven)	*messonairo*
waitress	la moza,	*mo-sa,*
	la mesera (Mex, CAm),	*messaira,*
	la garzona (Arg,	*garssona*
	Uru, Chi)	
wine	el vino	*veeno*
wine list	la carta de vinos	*karta deh veenoss*

A table for one, please
Una mesa para uno, por favor
oona meh-sa para oono por fa-vor

A table for two/three, please
Una mesa para dos/tres personas, por favor
oona meh-sa para doss/tress pairsonas por fa-vor

Do you have a set menu?
¿Hay menú/comida corriente (CAm)/comida corrida (Mex)?
i menoo/komeeda korr-yenteh/komeeda korreeda

Can we see the menu/wine list?
¿Nos trae la carta/la carta de vinos?
noss tra-eh la karta/la karta deh veenoss

What would you recommend?
¿Qué recomienda usted?
keh rekom-yenda oosteh

I'd like …
Quisiera …
keess-yaira

Just a coffee, please
Un café nada más, por favor
oon kafeh nada mass por fa-vor

A bottle of house red, please
Una botella de tinto de la casa, por favor
oona botay-ya deh teento deh la kassa por fa-vor

Two more beers, please
Otras dos cervezas/chops (Chi), por favor
o-trass doss sairveh-sass/chops por fa-vor

Waiter!/Waitress!
¡Señor!/¡Señorita!
sen-yor/sen-yoreeta

I didn't order this
No pedí esto
no pedee esto

May we have some more …?
¿Nos trae más …?
noss tra-eh mass

Can we have the bill, please?
¿Nos trae la cuenta, por favor?
noss tra-eh la kwenta por fa-vor

Can we pay separately?
Podemos pagar por separado
podeh-moss pagar por separado

That was a very good meal, thank you
La comida estuvo muy buena, gracias
la kommeeda estoovo mwee bweh-na grass-yass

My compliments to the chef!
¡Felicite al cocinero de mi parte!
feleesseeteh al kosseenairo deh mee parteh

> ### YOU MAY HEAR
>
> **¡Buen provecho!**
> Enjoy your meal!
>
> **¿Qué quiere tomar?**
> What would you like to drink?
>
> **¿La comida ha sido de su gusto?**
> Did you enjoy your meal?

MENU GUIDE

aceitunas	olives
acelgas	spinach beet
achicoria	chicory, endive
aguacate	avocado
agua de panela	drink made from water and sugar
agua mineral	mineral water
agua mineral con gas	fizzy mineral water
agua mineral sin gas	still mineral water
aguardiente	a clear spirit similar to brandy or white rum
ahumados	smoked fish
ají	chilli
ajiaco	stew of chicken, potatoes, vegetables and corn on the cob
ajo	garlic
albaricoques	apricots
albóndigas	meatballs
alcachofas	artichokes
alcaparras	capers
al clima	at room temperature
almejas	clams
almendras	almonds
almuerzo	set menu; lunch
al tiempo	at room temperature
alubias	beans
ananás	pineapple
anchoas	anchovies
anguila	eel
angulas	baby eels
anís	aniseed-flavoured spirit
anticuchos	beef kebabs
api	thick custard-like drink made from maize and cinnamon
arenque	herring
arepa	corn meal pancake
aromáticas	herb teas
arroz a la cubana	rice with fried eggs
arroz a la valenciana	rice with seafood
arroz con leche	rice pudding

arroz moro	rice with spiced meat (*Cub*)
arvejas	peas
asado	roast meat
asado de tira	spareribs
atole	thick oats-based drink
atún	tuna
avellanas	hazelnuts
azúcar	sugar
bacalao a la vizcaína	cod served with ham, peppers and garlic
bacalao al pil pil	cod served with chillis and garlic
baleada	corn meal pancake filled with beans, cheese and eggs
bandeja	main dish
bandeja paisa	beef, beans, eggs, rice and vegetables
batido	milk shake
bebidas	drinks
berenjenas	aubergines
besugo al horno	baked sea bream
bife	steak
bistec de ternera	veal steak
bizcochos	sponge fingers
blanquillos	eggs
bolillo	bread roll
bonito al horno	baked tuna fish
bonito con tomate	tuna with tomato
boquerones fritos	fried anchovies
borracho	cake soaked in rum
brazo de gitano	sponge cake rolled up with jam filling
brevas	figs
broqueta de riñones	kidney kebabs
budín	cake
budín inglés	trifle
buñuelos	light fried pastries; doughnuts
burritos	small pancakes with sauce
buseca	oxtail soup with peas and beans
butifarra	spicy blood sausage
cabrito asado	roast kid
cachelada	pork stew with tomatoes, onions and garlic
cachito	croissant
café	coffee
café americano	black coffee (*Mex*)
café con leche	white coffee

café cortado	coffee with a dash of milk
café de olla	coffee made with cinammon and raw sugar
café perico	coffee with a dash of milk
café perfumado	coffee with a dash of brandy or other spirits
café solo	black coffee
café tinto	black coffee *(Col)*
caguama	turtle
calabacín/calabacita	courgette
calabaza	pumpkin
calamares a la romana	squid rings in batter
calamares en su tinta	squid cooked in their ink
calamares fritos	fried squid
caldeirada	fish soup
caldereta gallega	vegetable stew
caldo de …	… soup
caldo de gallina	chicken soup
caldo de pescado	clear fish soup
caldo gallego	vegetable soup
caldo guanche	potato soup
callampas	mushrooms *(Chi)*
callos a la madrileña	tripe cooked with chillis
camarones	baby prawns
camote	sweet potato
canelones	canneloni
cangrejos de río	river crabs
caracoles	snails
caramelos	sweets
caraotas	beans
carne de chancho	pork
carne de res	beef
carnes	meat, meat dishes
carnitas	barbecued pork
carro de queso	cheese board
castañas	chestnuts
cazuela	stew
cazuela de mariscos	seafood stew
cebada	drink made from fermented barley
cebolla	onion
cebollitas	spring onions
cecina	corned beef
cena	dinner, evening meal

centollo	spider crab
cerezas	cherries
cerveza	beer
ceviche	marinated raw seafood cocktail
chairo	mutton and potato broth
champiñones	mushrooms
chancho	pork
chanquetes	fish similar to whitebait
chauchas	green beans
chayote	vegetable similar to marrow or squash
chicha	drink made from maize, usually alcoholic
chícharos	peas
chicharrón	pork crackling
chifa	Chinese food
chile	chilli pepper
chile poblano	green pepper (Mex)
chiles rellenos	stuffed peppers
chipirones	squid
chipotle	dark chilli sauce
chirimoya	custard apple, soursop – green heart-shaped fruit with white flesh
chirmol	hot sauce made from tomatoes, onion and mint
chivito	steakburger (Uru)
choclo	maize, corn on the cob, sweet corn
chocolate santafereño	hot chocolate and cheese (Bol)
chocos	squid
cholgas	mussels
chongos	curd cheese in sweet syrup
chop	beer (Chi)
chuleta de …	… chop (cutlet)
chuletón	large chop (cutlet)
chuños	freeze-dried potatoes (Per, Bol)
chupete	lollipop
churisco	baked sausage
churrasco	roast and grilled meats
churros	deep-fried pastry
cigalas	crayfish
cilantro	coriander
ciruelas	plums
ciruelas pasas	prunes
clérico	wine, fruit and fruit juice

cochinillo asado	roast suckling pig
cocido	stew made with meat, chickpeas or chicken
coco	coconut
cóctel de mariscos	seafood cocktail
codornices	quail
col	cabbage
cola de mono	eggnog (Chi)
colecillas de Bruselas	Brussels sprouts
coliflor	cauliflower
comal	griddle
comida	set menu; evening meal
comida corrida	set menu (Mex)
comida corriente	set menu (CAm)
completo	hot-dog
conejo	rabbit
conejo asado	roast rabbit
congrio	conger eel
coñac	brandy
copa de helado	assorted ice cream
cordero	lamb
cordero asado	roast lamb
cordero chilindrón	lamb stew
costillas de cerdo	pork ribs
cotufa	Jerusalem artichoke
crema catalana	crème brûlée
cremada	dessert made with eggs and butter
crema de espárragos	cream of asparagus soup
crepa	sweet pancake
criadillas	bull's testicles
criadillas de tierra	truffles
crocante	ice cream with chopped nuts
croquetas	croquettes
croquetas de pescado	fish croquettes
cuajada	milk curds
cuitlacoche	type of edible mushroom which grows on the maize plant
culantro	coriander
curanto	combination dish of various meats, seafood and vegetables (Chi)
usuco	armadillo
cuy	guinea pig
damasco	apricot

dátiles	dates
desayuno	breakfast
dulce	sugar
durazno	peach
ejotes	runner beans
elote	maize, corn on the cob, sweet corn
embutidos	sausages
empanada	pasty filled with meat or fish
empanada santiaguesa	fish pie
empanadillas de bonito	tuna pasties
empanadillas de carne	meat pasties
enchilada	fried corn meal pancake filled with meat, vegetables, or cheese in sauce
endivias	endive, chicory
ensalada	salad
ensalada de frutas	fruit salad
ensalada de pollo	chicken salad
ensalada mixta	mixed salad
ensaladilla rusa	Russian salad – cold diced potatoes and other vegetables in mayonnaise
entrecot de ternera	veal entrecôte
entremeses de la casa	hors d'oeuvres, starters
epazote	herb tea (Mex)
escalope de ternera	veal escalope
escarola	curly endive
espada ahumado	smoked swordfish
espaguetis	spaghetti
espárragos	asparagus
espárragos con mayonesa	asparagus with mayonnaise
espinacas	spinach
espinacas a la crema	creamed spinach
espinazo de cerdo con patatas	stew of pork ribs with potatoes
estofado de ...	... stew
estofado de liebre	hare stew
estragón	tarragon
fabada (asturiana)	bean stew with sausage
faisán con castañas	pheasant with chestnuts
faisán estofado	stewed pheasant
fiambres	cold meats
fideos	thin pasta, noodles
filete a la parrilla	grilled beef
filete de cerdo	pork steak

filete de ternera	veal steak
flan	crème caramel
flan al ron	crème caramel with rum
flan de caramelo	crème caramel
flauta	corn meal pancake, filled with chicken
flor de calabaza	pumpkin flower
frambuesas	raspberries
fresas	strawberries
fresas con crema	strawberries and cream
fresco	fruit juice *(CAm)*
fresones	strawberries
frijoles	kidney beans
frijoles refritos	refried beans
fritada	scraps of fried meat
fritos con jamón	fried eggs with ham
fruta	fruit
fruta variada	assorted fresh fruit
frutas en almíbar	fruit in syrup
frutillas	strawberries
gallina	chicken
gallina en pepitoria	chicken stewed with peppers
gallo pinto	rice and beans *(CAm)*
gallos	corn meal pancakes filled with meat or chicken in sauce
gambas al ajillo	garlic prawns
gambas a la americana	prawns
gambas a la plancha	grilled prawns
gambas con mayonesa	prawns with mayonnaise
gambas en gabardina	prawns in batter
gambas rebozadas	prawns in batter
garbanzos	chickpeas
garbanzos a la catalana	chickpeas with sausage, boiled eggs and pine nuts
garobo	iguana
gazpacho andaluz	cold tomato soup
gelatina	jelly, jello
gol	alcoholic drink made from butter, sugar and milk *(Chi)*
gorditas	thick fried pancake with sauce
gratén de ...	... au gratin – baked in a cream and cheese sauce
grelo	turnip

guacamole	avocado dip
guanábana	custard apple, soursop – green heart-shaped fruit with white flesh
guarapo	rough liquor made from sugar cane
guayaba	guava – fruit with a green skin and sweet, pink flesh
guinda	black cherry; alcoholic drink made from black cherries
guindada/guindilla	cherry brandy
guineo	small banana
guisantes	peas
habas	broad beans
habas con jamón	broad beans with ham
habichuelas	beans
helado de chocolate	chocolate ice cream
helado de fresa	strawberry ice cream
helado de turrón	nut ice cream
helado de vainilla	vanilla ice cream
hígado	liver
hígado con cebolla	liver cooked with onion
hígado de ternera estofado	braised calves' liver
hígado estofado	braised liver
higos con miel y nueces	figs with honey and nuts
higos secos	dried figs
hongos	mushrooms
horchata (de chufas)	cold almond-flavoured milk
hormigas culonas	large fried ants
huachinango	red snapper
huevo hilado	egg yolk garnish
huevos a la flamenca	fried eggs with ham and tomato
huevos a la mexicana	scrambled eggs with peppers, onions and garlic
huevos cocidos	hard-boiled eggs
huevos con jamón	eggs with ham
huevos con panceta	eggs and bacon
huevos con papas fritas	fried eggs and chips
huevos con picadillo	eggs with minced (ground) sausage
huevos con salchichas	eggs and sausages
huevos duros	hard-boiled eggs
huevos duros con mayonesa	boiled eggs with mayonnaise
huevos escalfados	poached eggs
huevos fritos	fried eggs

huevos fritos con chorizo	fried eggs with Spanish sausage
huevos pasados por agua	soft-boiled eggs
huevos pericos	scrambled eggs
huevos rancheros	fried eggs with hot tomato sauce
huevos rellenos	stuffed eggs
huevos revueltos	scrambled eggs
huevos revueltos con tomate	scrambled eggs with tomato
humitas	sweet corn tamales
húngaro	hot-dog with spicy sausage in a white sauce
jaiba	crab
jalapeños	hot green chillis
jamón serrano	cured ham
jeta	pigs' cheeks
jícama	sweet turnip-like fruit eaten with lemon juice or chilli
jitomate	tomato
judías verdes	green beans
judías verdes con jamón	green beans with ham
jugo	fruit juice
jugo de damasco	apricot juice
jugo de durazno	peach juice
jugo de lima	lime juice
jugo de limón	lemon juice
jugo de naranja	orange juice
jugo de piña	pineapple juice
jugo de tomate	tomato juice
langosta	lobster
langosta a la americana	lobster with brandy and garlic
langosta fría con mayonesa	cold lobster with mayonnaise
langosta gratinada	lobster au gratin
langostinos a la plancha	grilled king prawns
langostinos con mayonesa	king prawns with mayonnaise
laurel	bay leaves
leche frita	pudding made from milk, eggs and semolina
leche merengada	cold milk with meringues
lechona	suckling pig
lechuga	lettuce
lengua de buey	ox tongue
lengua de cordero estofada	stewed lambs' tongue
lenguado a la parrilla	grilled sole

lenguado a la plancha	grilled sole
lenguado a la romana	sole in batter
lenguado frito	fried sole
lentejas	lentils
licores	spirits, liqueurs
licuado	milk shake
licuado de fresas	strawberry milk shake
liebre estofada	stewed hare
lima	lemon, lime
llapingachos	potato and cheese pancakes
locro	maize and meat soup
lombarda rellena	stuffed red cabbage
lombarda salteada	sautéed red cabbage
lomo	pork fillet
lomo curado	pork-loin sausage
lomo saltado	stir-fried pork with vegetables
lonchas de jamón	sliced, cured ham
longaniza	cooked spicy sausage
lubina a la marinera	sea bass in a parsley sauce
lubina al horno	baked sea bass
macarrones	macaroni
macarrones gratinados	macaroni cheese
macedonia de fruta	fruit salad
macho	large green banana
maíz	maize, sweet corn
malta	dark beer
malteada	milk shake
mamey	round, apple-sized tropical fruit with light-brown skin and sweet orange flesh
mandarinas	tangerines
maní/manises	peanuts
manitas de cordero	lamb shank
manos de cerdo	pigs' trotters
manteca	butter (Arg, Uru)
mantecadas	small sponge cakes
mantequilla	butter
manzanas	apples
manzanas asadas	baked apples
manzanilla	dry sherry-type wine
maracuyá	passion fruit
mariscada	cold mixed shellfish

mariscos del día	fresh shellfish
mariscos del tiempo	seasonal shellfish
masa	dough
matambre arrollado	rolled beef stuffed with spinach, onion, carrots and eggs
mate	bitter tea
mate de coca	coca leaf tea
mazápan	marzipan
medallones de anguila	eel steaks
medallones de merluza	hake steaks
media de agua	half-bottle of mineral water
mejillones	mussels
mejillones a la marinera	mussels in a wine sauce
melocotón	peach
melocotones en almíbar	peaches in syrup
membrillo	quince jelly
menestra de legumbres	vegetable stew
menú de la casa	set menu
menú del día	set menu
merengada	fruit juice with ice, milk and sugar
merluza a la parrilla	grilled hake
merluza a la plancha	grilled hake
merluza a la romana	hake steaks in batter
merluza en salsa	hake in sauce
merluza en salsa verde	hake in a parsley and wine sauce
merluza fría	cold hake
merluza frita	fried hake
mermelada	jam
mermelada de ciruelas	prune jam
mermelada de damasco	apricot jam
mermelada de durazno	peach jam
mermelada de frambuesas	raspberry jam
mermelada de fresas	strawberry jam
mermelada de naranja	orange marmalade
mero	grouper (type of fish)
mero a la parrilla	grilled grouper
mero en salsa verde	grouper in garlic and parsley
mezcal	spirit distilled from the maguey cactus
milanesa	breaded chop or escalope
mole	thick dark chilli sauce, or dessert made from banana and chocolate (*Gua*)

mollejas de ternera fritas	fried sweetbreads
mondongo	tripe
mora	blackberry
morcilla	black pudding
morros de cerdo	pigs' cheeks
morros de vaca	cows' cheeks
mortadela	salami-type sausage
morteruelo	type of mince pie
mosh	oats with cinammon and honey (Gua)
nabo	turnip
nacatamales	corn meal dough filled with meat in sauce and steamed in banana leaves
naranjas	oranges
natillas	cold custard
natillas de chocolate	cold custard with chocolate
níscalos	wild mushrooms
nísperos	medlars – fruit like crab apples
nixtamal	corn meal dough
nopalitos	pickled chopped cactus leaves
nueces	walnuts
orejas de cerdo	pigs' ears
ostras	oysters
otros mariscos según precios en plaza	other shellfish, depending on prices
pabellón	minced (ground) meat, beans, rice and banana (Ven)
pachamanca	traditional Peruvian dish of meats cooked in clay
pacumutu	beef kebabs
paella	fried rice with various meats
paella valenciana	rice with shellfish, chicken etc
paila	fried or poached eggs with bread
paleta de cordero lechal	shoulder of lamb
palta	avocado
pan	bread
pana	liver (Chi)
panache de verduras	vegetable stew
pan de higos	dried fig cake with cinnamon
pan dulce	buns and cakes
panceta	bacon

pancita	tripe
papa	potato
papa rellena	stuffed potato (Per)
papas a la criolla	potatoes in hot, spicy sauce
papas a la huancaína	stuffed potato (Per)
papas asadas	baked potatoes
papas bravas	potatoes in cayenne pepper
papas fritas	chips
papaya	papaya
pargo	fish
parrillada de caza	mixed grilled game
parrillada de mariscos	mixed grilled shellfish
pasas	raisins
pastel de …	… cake
pastel de ternera	veal pie
pasteles	cakes
pasticho	lasagne (Ven)
patacón	mashed potato and banana (Col)
patatas	crisps, potato chips
patín	tomato-based sauce
patitos rellenos	stuffed duckling
pato asado	roast duck
pato a la naranja	duck à l'orange
pato estofado	stewed duck
pavipollo	large chicken
pavo asado	roast turkey
pavo relleno	stuffed turkey
pecho de ternera	breast of veal
pechuga de pollo	breast of chicken
pepián	meat stew
pepinillos	gherkins
pepinillos en vinagreta	gherkins in vinaigrette sauce
pepino	cucumber
peras	pears
percebes	edible barnacles
perdices	partridges
perdices asadas	roast partridges
perdices con chocolate	partridges with chocolate
perejil	parsley
pescaditos fritos	fried fish
pestiños	sugared pastries
píbil	dark sauce

picadillo	minced meat, ground meat
picadillo de ternera	minced veal, ground veal
picante/picoso	hot, spicy
pichón	pigeon
piloncillo	raw sugar
pimienta	black pepper
pimientos a la riojana	baked red peppers fried in oil
pimientos fritos	fried peppers
pimientos morrones	strong peppers
pimientos rellenos	stuffed peppers
pimientos verdes	green peppers
pinchitos	snacks served in bars
pincho	kebab
pinchos morunos	kebabs
pinolillo	alcoholic drink made from toasted seeds
piña fresca	fresh pineapple
piñones	pine nuts
pipián	hot chilli sauce
pique macho	chopped beef with onions
pisco	clear spirit made from grapes
pisco sour	drink made from pisco, lemon juice and egg whites
pisto	fried mixed vegetables
pisto manchego	marrow with onion and tomato
pitahaya	red fruit of a cactus plant with soft, sweet flesh
plátanos	bananas
plátanos flameados	flambéed bananas
plato montañero	beef, sausage, beans, eggs and rice
poblano	green pepper (Mex)
pollo al ajillo	fried chicken with garlic
pollo a la parrilla	grilled chicken
pollo al vino blanco	chicken in white wine
pollo asado	roast chicken
pollo braseado	braised chicken
pollo con tomate	chicken with tomatoes
pollo con verduras	chicken and vegetables
pollo en cacerola	chicken casserole
pollo en pepitoria	chicken in wine with saffron, garlic and almonds
pollo salteado	sautéed chicken

polvorones	sugar-based dessert
pomelo	grapefruit
porotos	kidney beans
postre	dessert
potaje	thick broth
potaje de garbanzos	chickpea stew
pozole	maize and meat stew
puchero canario	meat casserole with chickpeas
puerco chuk	pork stew
pulpitos con cebolla	baby octopus with onions
pulpo	octopus
pulque	thick alcoholic drink distilled from the pulp of the agave cactus (*Mex*)
pupusa	dumpling usually filled with cheese or meat (*CAm*)
puré de papas	mashed potatoes, potato purée
puro de caña	sugar cane liquor
purrusalda	cod with leeks and potatoes
queque	cake
quesadilla	fried corn meal pancake usually filled with cheese or meat
queso	cheese
queso del país	local cheese
queso de oveja	sheep cheese
quisquillas	shrimps
rábanos	radish
ragout de ternera	veal ragoût
rajas	grilled green peppers
rape a la cazuela	stewed monkfish
rape a la plancha	grilled monkfish
raya	skate
redondo al horno	roast fillet of beef
refresco	soft drink, fizzy drink
refritos	refried beans
remolacha	beetroot
repollo	cabbage
repostería de la casa	cakes baked on the premises
requesón	cream cheese, cottage cheese
res	beef
riñones	kidneys
riñones al jerez	kidneys with sherry
róbalo	bass

rocoto	hot red pepper
rodaballo	turbot
romero	rosemary
ron	rum
ropa vieja	shredded meat
rosca	traditional sponge cake
roscas	sweet pastries
saice/saisi	spicy meat broth (Bol)
sajta	chicken in hot sauce (Bol)
sal	salt
salchichas	sausages
salchichón	white sausage with pepper
salmón ahumado	smoked salmon
salmón a la parrilla	grilled salmon
salmonetes	red mullet
salmonetes a la parrilla	grilled red mullet
salmonetes en papillote	red mullet cooked in foil
salmón frío	cold salmon
salmorejo	thick sauce made with bread
salpicón de mariscos	shellfish with vinaigrette
salsa ali oli/allioli	mayonnaise with garlic
salsa bechamel	white sauce
salsa de tomate	tomato sauce
salsa holandesa	hollandaise sauce
salsa mahonesa/mayonesa	mayonnaise
salsa tártara	tartare sauce
salsa verde	hot sauce with chilli and tomatoes
salsa vinagreta	vinaigrette sauce
salteño	small pasty usually filled with chicken or other meat and sauce
sancocho	vegetable soup with meat or fish
sandía	water melon
sangría	sangría – mixture of red wine, lemon juice, sugar and fruit
sardinas a la brasa	barbecued sardines
sardinas a la parrilla	grilled sardines
sardinas fritas	fried sardines
seco	dry; main dish
seco de ...	... stew
semidulce	medium-sweet
sesos	brains
setas	mushrooms

sidra	cider
silpancho	beef with eggs (*Bol*)
singani	grape spirit
sobreasada	soft red sausage with cayenne
solomillo frio	cold roast beef
solomillo con patatas	fillet steak with chips
solomillo de ternera	fillet of veal
sopa	soup
sopa de ajo	garlic soup
sopa de almendras	almond-based pudding
sopa de fideos	noodle soup
sopa de gallina	chicken soup
sopa del día	soup of the day
sopa de lentejas	lentil soup
sopa de marisco	fish and shellfish soup
sopa de mondongo	tripe stew (*Hon*)
sopa de pescado	fish soup
sopa de tortilla	soup with corn meal pancakes
sopa de verduras	vegetable soup
sopa mallorquina	soup with tomatoes and meat
sopa seca	rice course
sopa sevillana	fish and mayonnaise soup
sorbete	sorbet; ice cream (*CAm*); fruit juice with cream (*Col*)
soufflé de queso	cheese soufflé
surubí	a freshwater fish
taco	corn meal pancake usually filled with beef or chicken
tajadas	fried banana strips
tallarines	noodles
tallarines a la italiana	tagliatelle
tamales	corn meal dough filled with meat and sauce then steamed in banana leaves
tamarindo	tamarind
tapado	stew
tarta de almendra	almond gâteau
tarta de chocolate	chocolate gâteau
tarta de fresas	strawberry tart or gâteau
tarta de manzana	apple tart
tarta helada	ice-cream gâteau
tarta moca	mocha tart

tequila	alcohol distilled from the pulp of the agave cactus (*Mex*)
ternera asada	roast veal
tocino	bacon
tomates rellenos	stuffed tomatoes
tomillo	thyme
tordo	thrush
toronja	grapefruit
torrejas	French toast
torrijas	sweet pastries
torta	cake, pie; filled roll (*Mex*)
tortilla	corn meal pancake
tortilla de harina	wheat flour pancake
tortilla de huevo	omelette
tostadas	fried crisp pancake with sauce
trucha ahumada	smoked trout
trucha con jamón	trout with ham
truchas molinera	trout meunière – trout dipped in flour, fried and served with butter, lemon juice and parsley
tuna	prickly pear
tuntas	freeze-dried potatoes (*Gua*)
turrón	nougat
turrón de Jijona	soft nougat
uvas	grapes
vainitas	green beans
vieiras	scallops
vino blanco	white wine
vino rosado	rosé wine
vino tinto	red wine
vuelvealavida	marinated seafood cocktail with chilli
yaguarlocro	potato soup with sausage
yerba mate	herbal tea
yuca	cassava
zanahorias	carrots
zapallo	marrow, squash
zapote	sweet pumpkin
zarzamoras	blackberries
zarzuela de mariscos	seafood stew

SHOPS AND SERVICES

This chapter covers all sorts of shopping needs and services, and to start with you'll find some general phrases which can be used in lots of different places – many of which are named in the list below. After the general phrases come some more specific requests and sentences to use when you've found what you need, be it food, clothing, repairs, film-developing, a haircut or haggling in the market. Don't forget to refer to the mini-dictionary for items you may be looking for.

Shop hours vary considerably from country to country and region to region; in hot areas, for example, shops may often open very early in the morning then close until late afternoon or early evening. In the major cities, shops will usually remain open until 8pm but may close for lunch between 1 and 4pm. The majority of shops and stores are closed on Sundays.

Toiletries and non-drug items can be bought from supermarkets and department stores; medicines and drugs are only sold in a **farmacia**. (See Health page 110 for details about pharmacies.)

Much shopping in Latin America will be done in markets where prices are variable and bargaining is common. You should ask whether the price is fixed '**¿Es precio fijo?**' (*ess press-yo fee-HO*) and if the answer is ambiguous, bargaining can then begin.

USEFUL WORDS AND PHRASES

bag	una bolsa	*bolsa*
bakery	la panadería	*panadairee-a*
(*selling cakes*)	la pastelería	*pasteh-lairee-a*
bookstore	la librería	*leebrairee-a*
butcher's shop	la carnicería	*karneesairee-a*
buy	comprar	*komprar*
cake shop	la pastelería	*pasteh-lairee-a*
camera shop	la tienda fotográfica	*tyenda fotografeeka*
camping equipment	equipos de camping	*ekeeposs deh kampeen*

cashier	la caja	_ka-Ha_
cheap	barato	_bara-to_
confectionery shop	la dulcería, la confitería	_doolssairee-a, konfeetairee-a_
craft shop	la tienda de artesanías	_tyenda deh artessanee-ass_
department store	los grandes almacenes	_grandess almasseh-ness_
dry cleaner	la tintorería	_teentoreree-a_
electrical goods store	la tienda de electrodomésticos	_tyenda deh elektrodomesteekoss_
expensive	caro	_ka-ro_
fish shop	la pescadería	_peskadairee-a_
gift shop	la tienda de regalos	_tyenda deh rega-loss_
greengrocer's	la frutería	_frooteree-a_
grocery store	el almacén, la tienda de abarrotes/alimentos,	_alma-sen, tyenda deh abar-rotes/aleemen-toss,_
	el boliche (Chi, Arg, Uru),	_bolee-cheh,_
	la pulpería (Cos, ElS),	_poolpairee-a,_
	la bodega (Gua, Nic)	_bodeh-ga_
hairdresser's	la peluquería	_pelookairee-a_
hardware store	la ferretería,	_ferreh-tairee-a,_
	la tlapalería (Mex)	_tlap-alairee-a_
jewellery shop	la joyería	_Hoy-airee-a_
ladies' wear	ropa de señoras	_ro-pa deh sen-yorass_
launderette	la lavandería automática	_lavanderee-a owto-mateeka_
market	el mercado,	_mairkado,_
	la feria (Arg, Uru),	_fairee-a,_
	el tianguis (Mex)	_tyan-gees_
menswear	ropa de hombres	_ro-pa deh om-bress_
newsstand	el puesto de periódicos	_pweh-sto deh pairee-odeekoss_
optician's	la óptica	_opteeka_
receipt	el recibo	_resseebo_

record store	la discoteca	*deeskoteh-ka*
sale	rebajas,	*reba-Hass,*
	liquidación,	*leekeedass-yon,*
	gangas (*Mex*)	*gan-gass*
shoe repairs	reparación de	*reparass-yon deh*
	calzado	*kalssado*
shoe shop	la zapatería	*sapatairee-a*
shop	la tienda, el almacén	*tyenda, alma-sen*
shopping centre	el centro comercial	*sentro komairss-yal*
souvenir shop	la tienda de regalos	*tyenda deh rega-loss*
stationery store	la papelería	*papeh-lairee-a*
store	la tienda, el almacén	*tyenda, alma-sen*
supermarket	el supermercado	*soopermairkado*
tailor	la sastrería	*sastrairee-a*
till	la caja	*ka-Ha*
tobacco store	la tabaquería	*tabakairee-a*
toyshop	la juguetería	*Hoogheh-tairee-a*
travel agency	la agencia de viajes	*aHenssee-a deh vya-Hess*

Excuse me, where is/are …? (*in a supermarket*)
Disculpe, ¿dónde está/están …?
deesskoolpeh dondeh esta/estan

Where is there a … (shop)?
¿Dónde hay una (tienda de) …?
dondeh I oona tyenda deh

Where is the … department?
¿Dónde está la sección de …?
dondeh esta la sekss-yon deh

Is there a market here?
¿Hay un mercado/una feria (*Arg, Uru*)/un tianguis (*Mex*) aquí?
I oon mairkado/oona fairee-a/oon tyan-gees akee

I'd like …
Quisiera …
keess-yaira

83

Do you have …?
¿Tienen …?
tyeh-nen

How much is this?
¿Cuánto vale esto?
kwanto va-leh esto

Where do I pay?
¿Dónde se paga/se cobra?
dondeh seh paga/seh ko-bra

Do you take credit cards?
¿Puedo pagar con tarjeta de crédito?
pweh-do pagar kon tarHeh-ta deh kredeeto

I think perhaps you've short-changed me
Me parece que me ha dado cambio de menos
meh pareh-seh keh meh a dado kamb-yo deh menoss

Can I have a receipt?
¿Me puede dar recibo?
meh pweh-deh dar resseebo

Can I have a bag, please?
¿Me da una bolsa, por favor?
meh da oona bolsa por fa-vor

I'm just looking
Sólo estoy mirando
so-lo estoy meerando

I'll come back later
Regresaré luego
reh-gressareh lweh-go

Do you have any more of these?
¿Tiene más de éstos?
tyeh-neh mass deh estoss

Do you have anything cheaper?
¿Tiene algo más barato?
tyeh-neh algo mass barato

Do you have anything larger/smaller?
¿Tiene algo más grande/pequeño?
tyeh-neh algo mass grandeh/peh-ken-yo

Can I try it (them) on?
¿Puedo probármelo(s)?
pweh-do probarmeh-lo(ss)

Does it come in other colours?
¿Lo hay en otros colores?
lo i en otross koloress

It's too big/small for me
Me queda grande/pequeño
meh keh-da grandeh/peh-ken-yo

Could you gift-wrap it for me?
¿Podría envolvérmelo para regalo?
podree-a emvol-vairmeh-lo para rega-lo

I'd like to exchange this, it's faulty
Quiero que me cambien esto porque tiene un defecto
kyairo keh meh kamb-yen esto por-keh tyeh-neh oon defekto

I'm afraid I don't have the receipt
Lo lamento, no tengo el recibo
lo lamentoh, no tengo el resseebo

Can I have a refund?
¿Pueden reembolsarme (el dinero)?
pweh-den reh-embolsarmeh (el deenairo)

Where can I get this mended?
¿Dónde me pueden arreglar esto?
dondeh meh pweh-den arreh-glar esto

Can you mend this?
¿Puede repararme esto?
pweh-deh reh-pararmeh esto

I'd like this skirt/these trousers dry-cleaned
Quisiera que me limpien esta falda/estos pantalones
keess-yaira keh meh leemp-yen esta falda/estoss pantalo-ness

I'd like to make an appointment
Quiero hacer una cita
kyairo assair oona seeta

I want a cut and blow-dry
Quisiera un corte y moldeado con secador de mano
keess-yaira oon korteh ee moldeh-ado kon sekador deh mano

Just a trim, please
Recórtemelo un poco solamente, por favor
rekorteh-meh-lo oon poko solamenteh por fa-vor

When does the market open?
¿A qué hora abre el mercado?
a keh ora seh a-breh el mairkado

What's the price per kilo?
¿Cuánto vale el kilo?
kwanto valeh el keelo

Is it a fixed price?
¿Es precio fijo?
ess press-yo fee-Ho

That's too much! I'll give you ...
¡Es mucho! Le doy ...
ess mootcho! leh doy

That's fine. I'll take it
Está bien. Me lo llevo
esta byen. meh lo yeh-vo

I'll have a piece of that cheese
Me da un pedazo de ese queso
meh da oon ped_a_sso deh _e_sseh k_eh_-so

About 250/500 grams
Como doscientos cincuenta/quinientos gramos
k_o_mo doss-y_e_ntoss seen-kw_e_nta/keen-y_e_ntoss gr_a_-moss

A kilo/half a kilo of apples, please
Un kilo/medio kilo de manzanas, por favor
oon k_ee_lo/m_eh_-dyo k_ee_lo deh manss_a_nass por fa-v_o_r

THINGS YOU'LL SEE

abarrotes	grocery store
abierto	open
agencia de viajes	travel agency
alimentos	groceries
alquiler	rental, hire
autoservicio	self-service
barato	cheap
bricolage	do-it-yourself supplies
caja	till, cashier
calidad	quality
calzados	shoe shop
carnicería	butcher's shop
cerrado	closed
cerrado por vacaciones	closed for holidays
cerramos los ...	closed on ...
droguería	drugstore
ferretería	hardware store
flores	flowers
ganga	bargain
grandes almacenes	department store
hagalousted mismo	do-it-yourself
helados	ice creams

→

juguetes	toys
lavado de pelo	shampoo
librería	bookstore
liquidación total	stock clearance
moda	fashion
moldeado con secador de mano	blow-dry
mueblería/muebles	furniture store
no se admiten devoluciones	no refunds given
no tocar	do not touch
oferta	special offer
panadería	bakery
papelería	stationery store
pastelería	cake shop
peluquería de hombres	men's hairdresser
peluquería de señoras	ladies' hairdresser
planta inferior	lower floor
planta superior	upper floor
por favor, use una cesta/ un carrito	please take a basket/trolley
precio	price
rebajado	reduced
rebajas	bargains
rebajas de verano	summer sale
revelado	developing
ropa de hombres	menswear
saldos	sales
salón de peluquería	hairdressing salon
sección	department
señoras	ladies' department
sorbete	ice cream, fruit juice with cream (Col)
tabaquería	tobacco store
tintorería	dry cleaner

→

tlapalería	hardware store
ultramarinos	grocery store
venta	sale
verduras	vegetables

THINGS YOU'LL HEAR

¿Le están atendiendo?
Are you being served?

¿Qué desea?/¿Qué se le ofrece?
Can I help you?

¿No tiene suelto/sencillo?
Haven't you anything smaller? *(money)*

Lo siento, se nos han terminado
I'm sorry, we're out of stock

Esto es todo lo que tenemos
This is all we have

No podemos devolver el importe/el dinero
We cannot give cash refunds

¿Desea algo más?
Will there be anything else?

¿Cuánto quisiera?
How much would you like?

¿Le importa que sea un poco más?
Does it matter if it's a bit over?

Lo siento, no aceptamos tarjetas de crédito
I'm afraid we don't take credit cards

¿Cómo quiere que se lo corte?
How would you like it cut?

SPORT

Football (**el fútbol**) dominates the Latin American sporting scene, from north to south. But every other sport has its adherents and its practitioners throughout Latin America. In Cuba and Central America, for example, baseball (**el béisbol**) is almost more important than soccer. And in Mexico, American football (**el fútbol americano**) is popular, particularly among students. Every country other than landlocked Bolivia and Paraguay has its beaches or access to the sea, and although newer water sports such as sailboarding are still largely restricted to the resorts frequented by foreign tourists, you'll be able to go snorkelling or underwater fishing in many places. Argentina and Uruguay have equestrian sports of every kind; polo, is, however, entirely restricted to the wealthier classes. Chile's mountainous landscape has allowed the development of skiing and mountaineering. Golf, while it is played everywhere, is largely inaccessible to any but the better-off local people.

The Spanish legacy remains in both the wall game (**pelota** or **jai alai**) and in the bullfight (**los toros**). The latter is still popular in parts of Latin America although it is conducted in slightly different ways from Spain. In Central America the bullfights are less ritual and often more direct, as amateur fighters tackle the bulls.

USEFUL WORDS AND PHRASES

American football	el fútbol americano	_footbol amairee-kano_
athletics	el atletismo	_atleh-teessmo_
badminton	el badminton	_badmeenton_
ball	la pelota, el balón	_peh-lota, balon_
baseball	el béisbol	_bayssbol_
basketball	el básquet, el baloncesto	_bassket, balonsesto_
bicycle	una bicicleta	_beesseekleh-ta_
boxing	el box	_boks_

bullfight	los toros	_toross_
canoe	una piragua,	_peeragwa,_
	una canoa	_kano-a_
canoeing	el piragüismo	_peerag-weessmo_
cycling	el ciclismo	_seekleessmo_
diving board	un trampolín	_trampoleen_
fishing	la pesca	_peska_
fishing rod	una caña de pescar	_kan-ya deh peskar_
flippers	las aletas	_aleh-tass_
football (ball)	el balón	_balon_
(soccer)	el fútbol sóccer	_footbol sokair_
football match	un partido de fútbol	_parteedo deh footbol_
goggles	las gafas de bucear	_gafass deh boosseh-ar_
golf	el golf	_'golf'_
golf course	un campo de golf	_kampo deh golf_
hang-gliding	el ala delta	_ala delta_
horse racing	las carreras de	_kar-rairass deh_
	caballos	_kaba-yoss_
hunting	la caza	_kassa_
motor racing	las carreras de autos	_kar-rairass deh owtoss_
mountaineering	el andinismo	_andeeneessmo_
oxygen bottles	las botellas de	_botay-yass deh_
	oxígeno	_oksee-Heno_
pedal boat	un hidropedal	_eedropedal_
racket	una raqueta	_rakeh-ta_
ride (horse)	montar a caballo	_montar a kaba-yo_
riding	la equitación	_ekeetass-yon_
rock climbing	la escalada en rocas	_esskalada en rokass_
sail (noun)	la vela	_veh-la_
(verb)	navegar (a vela)	_navegar a veh-la_
sailboard	una tabla de	_tabla deh_
	windsurfing	_weendsoorfeen_
sailing	vela	_veh-la_
skin diving	el submarinismo	_soobmaree-neessmo_
snorkel	el respirador	_respeera-dor_
sports centre	el centro deportivo	_sentro deporteevo_

stadium	el estadio	*estad-yo*
surfboard	la tabla de surfing	*tabla deh soorfeen*
swim	nadar	*nadar*
swimming pool	la alberca	*albairka*
tennis	el tenis	*teh-neess*
tennis court	una cancha de tenis	*kancha deh teh-neess*
tennis racket	una raqueta de tenis	*rakeh-ta deh teh-neess*
underwater fishing	la pesca submarina	*peska soobmareena*
volleyball	el voleibol	*volay-bol*
water-skiing	el esquí acuático	*eskee akwateeko*
water-skis	los esquís acuáticos	*eskeess akwateekos*
go windsurfing	hacer windsurfing	*assair weendsoorfeen*
wrestling	la lucha libre	*lootcha leebreh*
yacht	un yate	*ya-teh*

How do I get to the beach?
¿Cómo llego a la playa?
komo yeh-go a la pla-ya

How deep is the water here?
¿Qué profundidad tiene el agua aquí?
keh profoondee-da tyeh-neh el agwa akee

Is it safe to swim here?
¿Se puede nadar sin peligro aquí?
seh pweh-deh nadar seen pelee-gro akee

Can I fish here?
¿Puedo pescar aquí?
pweh-do peskar akee

I would like to rent a bicycle
Quisiera alquilar una bicicleta
keess-yaira alkeelar oona beeseekleh-ta

How much does it cost per hour/day?
¿Cuánto vale la hora/el día?
kwanto valeh la ora/el dee-a

I would like to take water-skiing lessons
Quisiera tomar clases de esquí acuático
keess-yaira tomar klasess deh eskee akwateeko

Where can I rent …?
¿Dónde puedo alquilar …?
dondeh pweh-do alkeelar

I haven't played this before
Nunca había jugado esto
noonka abee-a Hoogado esto

What's the score?
¿A cómo van?
a komo van

THINGS YOU'LL SEE

acceso playa	to the beach
alberca	swimming pool
alquiler de botes	boats to rent
alquiler de sombrillas	sunshades to rent
alquiler de tablas	board hire
alquiler de tumbonas	deckchairs to rent
autódromo	motor racing track
balneario	swimming pool; resort
cancha de tenis	tennis court
corriente peligrosa	dangerous current
hipódromo	racetrack *(horses)*
peligro	danger
piscina	swimming pool
prohibido bañarse	no swimming
prohibido pescar	no fishing
socorrista	lifeguard
velódromo	cycle track

POST OFFICES AND BANKS

Post Offices in Latin America deal only with mail and telegrams, so don't look for a phone there; use a call box or find the telephone exchange (see Telephones page 99). Stamps (**estampillas**) can be bought in the post office or in some shops, for example stationery stores and bookstores. In some post offices you may pay the postage and have the item franked (**franqueado**) instead of buying a stamp. You can also send parcels from a separate counter at the post office; they should be registered (**certificado**), especially if they are being sent abroad. Sometimes parcels sent outside the country need to be passed by customs (**la aduana**).

Bank opening hours vary from country to country, but normally they are open Monday to Friday from 8 or 8.30am to 1 or 1.30pm, and from 2 to 4.30pm. Nevertheless, you will need to check in each area. Foreign exchange counters (**cambios**) in banks are sometimes only open in the morning. On Saturday mornings larger banks in city centres may sometimes open, usually until 12.30pm. Each transaction in the bank will normally be carried out at a different window, and you may often be passed from one to the other. At the exchange window, for example, you may be given a form to take to the cashier (**la caja**). Each window, of course, has its own separate queue. Bear in mind that many people are paid their salaries through the bank, and, on pay day (the first of the month for example) the banks will often be very crowded. Cash dispensers are becoming more common, however.

USEFUL WORDS AND PHRASES

airmail	correo aéreo	*korreh-o a-aireh-o*
bank	el banco	*banko*
banknote	un billete de banco	*bee-yeh-teh deh banko*
cash	dinero	*deenairo*
cash dispenser	el cajero automático	*ka-Hairo owtomateeko*

change (*noun*)	sencillo, suelto	*sensee-yo, swelto*
(*verb*)	cambiar	*kamb-yar*
cheque	un cheque	*cheh-keh*
cheque book	el libro de cheques,	*leebro deh cheh-kess,*
	la chequera	*cheh-kayra*
credit card	la tarjeta de crédito	*tarHeh-ta deh*
		kredeeto
customs form	el impreso para la	*eempreh-so para la*
	aduana	*adwana*
delivery	el reparto	*reh-parto*
deposit (*noun*)	un ingreso	*eengreh-so*
dollar (*US*)	el dólar	*dolar*
exchange rate	el tipo de cambio	*teepo deh kamb-yo*
fax (*noun*)	un fax	*faks*
(*verb*)	mandar por fax	*mandar por faks*
form	un impreso	*eempreh-so*
international	un giro	*Heero eentairnass-*
money order	internacional	*yonal*
letter	una carta	*karta*
money order	un giro (postal)	*Heero postal*
package, parcel	un paquete	*pakeh-teh*
post (*noun*)	el correo	*korreh-o*
(*verb*)	echar al buzón	*etchar al boosson*
postage rates	las tarifas postales	*tareefass postaless*
postal order	un giro postal	*Heero postal*
post box	el buzón	*boosson*
postcard	una postal	*postal*
postcode	la zona postal	*sona postal*
poste-restante	la lista de correos	*leesta deh*
		korreh-oss
postman	el cartero	*kartairo*
post office	(la oficina de)	*offeesseena deh*
	Correos	*korreh-oss*
pound sterling	la libra esterlina	*leebra esterleena*
registered letter	una carta	*karta*
	certificada	*sairteefee-kada*

stamp	una estampilla,	*estampee-ya,*
	un timbre (Mex)	*teembreh*
surface mail	correo terrestre	*korreh-o*
		tair-restreh
telegram	un telegrama	*teleh-grama*
traveller's cheque	un cheque de	*cheh-keh deh*
	viajero	*vya-Hairo*
withdrawal	una retirada	*reteerada*

How much is a letter/postcard to England?
¿Cuánto vale la estampilla para una carta/una postal a Inglaterra?
kwanto valeh la estampee-ya para oona karta/oona postal a eenglaterra

I would like three 200 peso stamps
Quisiera tres timbres de doscientos pesos
keess-yaira tress teembress deh doss-syentoss peh-soss

I want to register this letter
Quiero mandar esta carta certificada
kyairo mandar esta karta sairteefee-kada

I want to send this package to Canada
Quiero mandar este paquete a Canadá
kyairo mandar esteh pakeh-teh a kanada

How long does the post to America take?
¿Cuánto demora el correo para Estados Unidos?
kwanto deh-mora el korreh-o para estadoss ooneedoss

Is there any mail for me?
¿Hay correo para mí?
i korreh-o para mee

I'd like to send a telegram/a fax
Quisiera mandar un telegrama/un fax
kveess-yaira mandar oon teleh-grama/oon fax

This is to go airmail
Quiero mandar esto por correo aéreo
ky<u>ai</u>ro mand<u>a</u>r <u>e</u>sto por korr<u>eh</u>-o a-<u>ai</u>reh-o

I'd like to change this into pesos
Quisiera cambiar esto por pesos
keess-y<u>ai</u>ra kamb-y<u>a</u>r <u>e</u>sto por p<u>eh</u>-soss

Can I cash these traveller's cheques?
Puedo cambiar estos cheques de viajero
pw<u>eh</u>-do kamb-y<u>a</u>r <u>e</u>stoss ch<u>eh</u>-kess deh vya-<u>H</u>airo

Can I have it in 5,000 peso notes, please?
¿Me lo puede dar en billetes de cinco mil pesos, por favor?
meh lo pw<u>eh</u>-deh dar en bee-y<u>eh</u>-tess deh s<u>ee</u>nko meel p<u>eh</u>-soss por fa-v<u>o</u>r

Could you give me smaller notes?
¿Podría darme billetes más pequeños?
podr<u>ee</u>-a d<u>a</u>rmeh bee-y<u>eh</u>-tess mass peh-k<u>e</u>n-yoss

Where should I sign?
¿Dónde firmo?
d<u>o</u>ndeh f<u>ee</u>rmo

→

cuentas corrientes	current accounts
destinatario	addressee
dirección	address
estampilla	stamp
extranjero	postage abroad
firma	signature
franqueo	franking
giros	money orders
horas de oficina	opening hours
horas de recogida	collection times
ingresos	deposits
lista de correos	poste-restante
localidad	place
paquetes	parcels, packages
plata	money
postal	postcard
rellenar	to fill in
remitente	sender
tarifa	charge
timbre	stamp
tipo de cambio	exchange rate
venta de estampillas	stamps
zona postal (Z.P.)	postcode

TELEPHONES

The telephone in Latin America is a source of constant frustration; in the major cities of most countries you can usually dial direct to the United States and Canada and to some places in Europe. But the situation differs from country to country, and outside the cities telephones are a great deal less reliable. In recent years, the state-owned telephone companies have been privatised, so that in some countries the telephone system is run by several competing companies – complicating matters further. Generally speaking, however, long-distance telephoning needs to be done from the Central Telephone Exchange (**la central telefónica**) where cabins are available. These will be marked in different ways: **urbana/ciudad** for local calls; **interurbana/pais/interior** for calls to other places within the country; and **internacional** for international calls. The external dialling codes vary from country to country but 09 is often the international code dialled before the code for the country.

The Central Telephone Exchange is usually in the central square of a town, or nearby, and is often known by the name of the telephone company or its initials: **ENCOTEL** (Argentina), **ENTEL** (Bolivia, Peru), **TELECOM** (Colombia), **SETEL** (Ecuador), **CANTV** (Venezuela), **TELCOR** (Nicaragua), **EGT** (Guatemala), **Teléfonos** (Mexico and elsewhere).

Not every country in Latin America has facilities for collect calls abroad. Neither Cuba nor Venezuela has any service at all, while collect calls to Europe are not available, or are very restricted, in El Salvador, Ecuador, Bolivia and Guatamala. They are difficult to arrange in Paraguay and Uruguay. In Colombia the service is available only from private telephones. Elsewhere (Peru, Honduras, Nicaragua) it is available only from the telephone exchange. In Mexico, by contrast, international calls are so expensive that collect is positively recommended. The service in Chile is generally good, while in Argentina direct dialling for international calls is rarely available.

As well as the Central Telephone Exchange, there are public telephone booths in every country, but they are usually not very reliable. Most bars and restaurants have telephones for public use. Most public telephones use coins, though the rampant inflation of recent years means that the value of the coins keeps on changing. In Peru, tokens (**fichas**) are used, obtainable from street vendors and newspaper kiosks, while in Colombia the relevant coins can be bought in packets from the central post office and telephone exchange.

USEFUL WORDS AND PHRASES

busy	ocupado	*okoopado*
call (noun)	una llamada (telefónica)	*yamada teh-leh-fonika*
(verb)	llamar (por teléfono)	*yamar por teh-leffono*
cardphone	un teléfono de tarjeta	*teh-leffono deh tarHeh-ta*
code	el prefijo	*preh-fee-HO*
collect call	una llamada por cobrar	*yamada por kobrar*
dial	marcar (un número)	*markar oon noomairo*
dialling tone	la señal para marcar, el tono para marcar	*sen-yal para markar, tono para markar*
direct dialling	discado directo	*deeskado deerekto*
engaged	ocupado	*okoopado*
enquiries	información	*eenformass-yon*
extension	extensión, anexo (*Arg*), interno (*Mex*)	*ekstenss-yon, anekso, eentairno*
information	información	*eenformass-yon*
international	internacional	*eentairnass-yonal*
operator (man)	el operador	*opairador*
(woman)	la operadora	*opairadora*
phone booth	una cabina telefónica	*kabeena teleh-fonnika*
phonecard	una tarjeta de teléfono	*tarHeh-ta deh teh-leffono*

public telephone	un teléfono público	*teh-leffono poobleeko*
receiver	el aparato	*aparato*
switchboard	la central,	*sentral,*
	el conmutador,	*konmootador,*
	la centralita	*sentraleeta*
telephone	un teléfono	*teh-leffono*
telephone directory	la guía telefónica,	*gee-a teleh-fonnika,*
	el directorio	*deerektor-yo*
	(telefónico)	*teleh-fonniko*
telephone number	el número	*noomairo deh*
	de teléfono,	*teh-leffono,*
	el fono *(Chi)*	*fono*

Where is the nearest phone booth?
¿Dónde está el teléfono más cercano?
dondeh esta el teh-leffono mass sairkano

Is there a telephone directory?
¿Hay una guía telefónica?
I oona gee-a teleh-fonnika

Can I call abroad from here?
¿Puedo llamar al extranjero desde aquí?
pweh-do yamar al estran-Hairo desdeh akee

How much is a call to the US?
¿Cuánto cuesta la llamada a Estados Unidos?
kwanto kwesta la yamada a estadoss ooneedoss

I would like to call collect to …
Quisiera hacer una llamada por cobrar a …
keess-yaira assair oona yamada por kobrar a

Could you give me an outside line, please?
¿Me puede dar línea, por favor?
meh pweh-deh dar leeneh-a por fa-vor

(It's John) speaking
Habla (John)
abla John

Hello (*response*)

Diga
deega

Bueno (*Mex*)
bweh-no

Aló (*Ven*)
alo

Hola (*Col/Per/Arg*)
ola

Oigo (*Cub*)
oy-go

May I speak to Maria, please

Me comunica con María, por favor
meh komooneeka kon maree-a por fa-vor

Me pasa ... (*Mex*)
meh pasa ...

Me conecta ... (*Arg/Chi*)
meh konekta ...

Could Mr Lopez come to the phone?

¿Que atienda/se ponga el teléfono el Sr. López?
keh at-yenda/seh ponga el teh-leffono el sen-yor lopess

Do you know what time he (she) will be back?

¿No sabe a qué hora regresa?
no sabeh a keh ora reh-gressa

Extension 345, please

Extensión tres cuatro cinco, por favor
ekstenss-yon tress kwatro seenko por fa-vor

Anexo ... (*Arg*)
anekso ...

Interno ... (*Mex*)
eentairno ...

Will you tell him (her) that David called

Le dice por favor que llamó David
leh deesseh por fa-vor keh yamo David

May I leave a message?

¿Puedo dejar recado?
pweh-do deHar rekado

I'll call back later

Volveré a llamar mas tarde
volvaireh a yamar mass tardeh

Sorry, I've got the wrong number
Disculpe, me he equivocado de número
deeskoolpeh meh eh ekeevokado deh noomairo

You've got the wrong number
Se equivocó de número
seh ekeevoko deh noomairo

I've been cut off
Se (me) cortó la comunicación
seh meh korto la komooneekass-yon

THINGS YOU'LL SEE

América	Latin America
cabina telefónica	phone booth
centralita	switchboard
central telefónica	telephone exchange
ciudad	local
conmutador	switchboard
cospeles	telephone tokens
descolgar el aparato	lift receiver
EEUU	USA
ficha	token
fuera de servicio	out of order
guía telefónica	telephone directory
interior	long-distance
interurbana	long-distance
introducir monedas	insert coins
locutorio telefónico	phone booth
malogrado	out of order
marcar el número	dial the number
monedas	coins
no funciona	out of order
operadora	operator
páginas amarillas	yellow pages

→

país	long-distance
paso (de contador)	unit
prefijo	code
ranura	slot
Reino Unido	UK
reparaciones	faults service
servicio a través de operadora	dialling through the operator
servicio automático	direct dialling
urbano	local

REPLIES YOU MAY BE GIVEN

Diga/Bueno/Aló/Hola/Oigo
Hello

Está llamando
It's ringing

¿Quién habla?
Who's speaking?

¿De parte de quién?
Who shall I say is calling?

No está/No se encuentra
He (she) is not in

No cuelgue
Don't hang up

Están comunicando/Está ocupado
The line is busy

¿Con quién desea hablar?
Who would you like to speak to?

¿Mande?
Can I help you?/What can I do for you?

EMERGENCIES

Information on local health services can be obtained from tourist information offices and consulates or embassies. Each country has its own telephone numbers for fire, ambulance and police.

In case of sudden illness or accident, go to the nearest **centro médico**, **casa de socorro** (emergency first-aid centre) or clinic (**clínica**), or to a hospital emergency department (**urgencias**). If on the road, look for **un puesto de socorro**, which is also an emergency first-aid centre.

If you are the victim of a robbery or assault, you should report this to the police as soon as possible. Make sure that the report is written on the required forms and that it is signed, sealed and stamped by the authorities. It is unlikely that your property will be returned, but the document reporting the theft will be important, particularly if you have lost identity papers. Let your embassy know if you have lost your passport.

USEFUL WORDS AND PHRASES

accident	un accidente	akssee-denteh
ambulance	una ambulancia	amboolanss-ya
assault (noun)	asalto	assalto
(verb)	asaltar	assaltar
break down	tener una pana,	tenair oona pana,
	descomponerse	deskomponair-seh
breakdown	una pana,	pana,
	una descompostura	deskompostoora
breakdown recovery	el servicio de grúa	sairveess-yo deh groo-a
burglar	un ladrón	ladron
burglary	un robo, un atraco	robo, atrako
crash (noun)	un choque	chokeh
(verb)	chocar	chokar
emergency	una emergencia	emair-Henss-ya
emergency department	urgencias	oor-Henss-yass

fire	un incendio	*eenssend-yo*
fire brigade	el servicio de bomberos	*sairveess-yo deh bombaiross*
flood	una inundación	*eenoondass-yon*
hurt	lastimado	*lastee-mado*
injured	herido	*ereedo*
lose	perder	*pairdair*
pickpocket	un carterista	*kartaireesta*
police	la policía	*poleessee-a*
police station	la comisaría	*kommeessaree-a*
rob	robar	*robar*
steal	robar	*robar*
theft	un robo	*robo*
thief	un ladrón	*ladron*
tow	remolcar	*remolkar*

Help!
¡Socorro!/¡Auxilio!
sokorro/owkseel-yo

Look out!
¡Cuidado!/¡Abusado! *(Mex)*
kweedado/aboossado

This is an emergency!
¡Es una emergencia!
ess oona emair-Henss-ya

Get an ambulance!
¡Llame una ambulancia!
ya-meh oona amboolanss-ya

Please send an ambulance to …
Haga el favor de mandar una ambulancia a …
aga el fa-vor deh mandar oona amboolanss-ya a

Please come to …
Por favor vengan a …
por fa-vor vengan a

My address is …
Mi dirección es …
mee deerekss-yon ess

We've had a break-in
Nos robaron la casa
noss robaron la kassa

My car's been broken into
Me forzaron el coche
meh forssaron el kotcheh

There's a fire at …
Hay incendio en …
I eenssend-yo en

Someone's been injured/knocked down
Hay una persona herida/atropellada
I oona pairsona ereeda/atropeh-yada

My car has been stolen
Me robaron el auto/el carro (Mex)
meh robaron el owto/el karro

The registration number is …
El número de matrícula es el …
el noomero deh matreekoola ess el

I've lost my traveller's cheques
Se me extraviaron los cheques de viajero
seh meh estrav-yaron loss cheh-kess deh vya-Hero

I want to report a stolen credit card
Quiero denunciar el robo de una tarjeta de crédito
kyairo denoonss-yar el robo deh oona tarHeh-ta deh kredeeto

It was stolen from my room
Lo robaron de mi cuarto
lo robaron deh mee kwarto

I lost it in/at …
Lo perdí en …
lo pairdee en

My luggage has gone missing
Mi equipaje se ha perdido
mee ekeepa-Heh seh a pairdeedo

Has my luggage turned up yet?
¿Se ha vuelto a encontrar mi equipaje?
seh a vwelto a enkontrar mee ekeepa-Heh

I've had a crash
Choqué
chokeh

I've been mugged
Me asaltaron
meh assaltaron

I've been raped
Me violaron
meh vee-olaron

My son's missing
Mi hijo se ha extraviado
mee ee-Ho seh a estrav-yado

I've locked myself out of my house/room/car
Dejé la llave dentro de la casa/del cuarto/del auto
deh-Heh la ya-veh dentro deh la kassa/del kwarto/del owto

He's drowning
Se está ahogando
seh esta a-ogando

She can't swim
No sabe nadar
no sabeh nadar

THINGS YOU'LL SEE

abierto las 24 horas del día	open 24 hours
botiquín	first-aid box
casa de socorro	emergency first-aid centre
comisaría	police station
farmacia de guardia/turno	duty chemist, late-night pharmacy
incendio	fire
marque …	dial …
policía	police
policía de tránsito	traffic police
primeros auxilios	first-aid post
puesto de socorro	first-aid post
servicios de rescate	rescue services
socorrista	lifeguard
taller (mecánico)	garage
urgencias	accident and emergency department

THINGS YOU'LL HEAR

¿Cuál es su dirección?
What's your address?

Sus señas, por favor
Name and address, please

¿Dónde se encuentra usted ahora?
Where are you now?

¿Puede describirlo?
Can you describe it (him)?

¿A qué hora ocurrió?
At what time did it happen?

HEALTH

Most Latin American countries have both public and private health services. Tourists and travellers can normally gain access to public hospitals (**centro de salud**, **hospital general**, **centro médico**) but there will often be a charge for treatment and all drugs will have to be bought at a pharmacy (**farmacia**, **droguería**), which may well be expensive. The standard of facilities can vary greatly. Cuba is outstanding for the quality of its public medical care. In addition to public hospitals there are hospitals and clinics in the social security (**seguro social**) system which are normally restricted to members i.e. those who pay regular contributions from their wages or salaries. Private hospitals are less crowded, but expensive. You should, therefore, take out adequate medical insurance before you travel to Latin America.

It is wise to have a health and dental check before travelling and to check with your doctor which inoculations are recommended for the countries you intend to visit. You should carry with you Spanish translations of any repeat prescriptions you may need and a translation of a doctor's letter should you suffer from any chronic condition.

Self-prescription of drugs is extremely common in Latin America; over 50% of drugs are sold without prescription across the counter. The traveller should beware, and pay attention to 'use-by' dates on drugs and antibiotics.

The most common health problems are the effects of heat, cold and untreated water or milk. Visitors should use bottled or filtered water at all times, and drink only pasteurised milk. In the mountains above 3,000 metres, altitude sickness (**soroche**) is common, whereas at sea level in tropical areas insects are probably the greatest danger.

Useful Words and Phrases

ambulance	una ambulancia	*amboolanss-ya*
antibiotics	los antibióticos	*anteebee-yoteekoss*
appendicitis	una apendicitis	*apendeeseeteess*

appendix	el apéndice	*apendeesseh*
aspirin	una aspirina	*aspeereena*
asthma	asma	*asma*
backache	un dolor de espalda	*dolor deh espalda*
bandage	el vendaje	*venda-Heh*
bite (*by dog*)	una mordedura	*mordeh-doora*
(*by insect, snake*)	una picadura	*peekadoora*
bladder	la vejiga	*veh-Heega*
blister	una ampolla	*ampo-ya*
blood	la sangre	*sangreh*
burn	una quemadura	*keh-madoora*
cancer	el cáncer	*kansair*
chest	el pecho	*petcho*
chickenpox	la varicela	*vareeseh-la*
cold	un resfriado	*resfree-ado*
concussion	una conmoción	*konmoss-yon*
constipation	estreñimiento	*estren-yeem-yento*
contact lenses	las lentes de contacto	*lentess deh kontakto*
corn	un callo	*ka-yo*
cough	tos	*toss*
cut	una cortadura	*kortadoora*
dentist	el dentista,	*denteesta,*
	el odontólogo	*odontologo*
diabetes	la diabetes	*dee-abeh-tess*
diarrhoea	una diarrea	*dee-arreh-a*
diphtheria	la difteria	*deeftairee-a*
dizzy	mareado	*mareh-ado*
doctor	el médico	*medeeko*
dysentery	la disentería	*deessenteree-a*
earache	un dolor de oídos	*dolor deh o-eedoss*
fever	la fiebre	*fee-eh-breh*
filling	un empaste	*empasteh*
first aid	primeros auxilios	*preemaiross owkzeel-yoss*
flu	la gripe	*greepeh*
fracture	una fractura	*fraktoora*
German measles	la rubeola	*roobeh-ola*

glasses	las gafas, los anteojos	*gafass, anteh-oHoss*
haemorrhage	una hemorragia	*emoraH-ya*
hayfever	la fiebre del heno	*fee-eh-breh del eh-no*
headache	un dolor de cabeza,	*dolor deh kabessa,*
	una jaqueca	*Hakeh-ka*
heart	el corazón	*korasson*
heart attack	un infarto	*eemfarto*
hospital	el hospital	*ospeetal*
ill	enfermo	*emfairmo*
indigestion	una indigestión	*eendee-Hest-yon*
injection	una inyección	*een-yekss-yon*
itch	un picor,	*peekor,*
	un comezón	*komesson*
kidney	el riñón	*reen-yon*
lump	un bulto	*boolto*
malaria	el paludismo	*paloodeesmo*
measles	el sarampión	*saramp-yon*
migraine	una jaqueca	*Hakeh-ka*
mumps	las paperas	*papairass*
nausea	náuseas	*nowseh-ass*
nurse (*female*)	la enfermera	*enfairmaira*
(*male*)	el enfermero	*enfairmairo*
operation	una operación,	*opairass-yon,*
	una intervención	*eentairvenss-yon*
	quirúrgica	*keeroor-Heeka*
optician	el oculista	*okooleessta*
pain	un dolor	*dolor*
penicillin	la penicilina	*peneesseeleena*
pharmacy	la farmacia	*farmassee-a*
plaster (*sticky*)	una tirita	*teereeta*
plaster of Paris	la escayola	*eskayola*
pneumonia	una pulmonía	*poolmonee-a*
pregnant	embarazada	*embarrassada*
prescription	una receta	*resseh-ta*
rheumatism	el reúma	*reh-ooma*
scald	una quemadura	*keh-madoora*

scratch	un arañazo	*arran-yasso*
smallpox	la viruela	*veerweh-la*
sore throat	un dolor de garganta	*dolor deh garganta*
splinter	una astilla	*astee-ya*
sprain	una torcedura	*torsseh-doora*
sting	una picadura	*peeka-doora*
stomach	el estómago	*esto-mago*
sunstroke	la insolación	*eensollass-yon*
tonsils	las amígdalas	*ameegdalass*
toothache	un dolor de muelas	*dolor deh mweh-lass*
travel sickness	mareo	*mareh-o*
typhoid	la fiebre tifoidea	*fee-eh-breh teefo-eedeh-a*
ulcer	una úlcera	*oolssaira*
vaccination	la vacunación	*vakoonass-yon*
vomit	vomitar	*vommeetar*
whooping cough	la tos ferina	*toss faireena*
yellow fever	la fiebre amarilla	*fee-eh-breh amaree-ya*

I have a pain in my leg
Me duele la pierna
meh dweh-leh la pyairna

My eyes hurt
Me duelen los ojos
meh dweh-len loss o-HOSS

I don't feel well
No me encuentro bien
no meh enkwentro byen

I feel faint
Siento que me voy a desmayar
syento keh meh voy a desma-yar

I have nausea
Tengo náuseas
tengo nowseh-ass

It hurts here
Me duele aquí
meh dweh-leh akee

It's a sharp/dull pain
Es un dolor agudo/sordo
ess oon dolor agoodo/sordo

It's sore all the time
Es un dolor constante
ess oon dolor konstanteh

It only hurts now and then
Sólo me duele a ratos
solo meh dweh-leh a ratoss

It hurts when you touch it
Me duele al tocarlo
meh dweh-leh al tokarlo

It stings/It itches
Escuece/Me pica
esskweh-sseh/meh peeka

I have a temperature
Tengo fiebre
tengo fee-eh-breh

I need a prescription for …
Necesito una receta para …
nesseh-seeto oona resseh-ta para

I normally take …
Normalmente tomo …
normalmenteh tomo

I have high/low blood pressure
Tengo la presión alta/baja
tengo la press-yon alta/ba-нa

I'm allergic to …
Soy alérgico a …
soy allair-Heeko a

I have been inoculated against …
Me he vacunado contra …
meh eh vakoonado kontra

Have you got anything for …?
¿Tiene usted algo para …?
tyeh-neh oosteh algo para

Do I need a prescription for …?
¿Necesito receta para …?
nesseh-seeto resseh-ta para

I've lost a filling
Se me ha caído un empaste
seh meh a ka-eedo oon empasteh

Will he (she) be all right?
¿Estará bien?
estara byen

How is he (she)?
¿Cómo está?
komo esta

THINGS YOU'LL SEE

casa de socorro	first-aid centre
centro de salud	hospital, health centre
centro médico	hospital, health centre
consulta	doctor's surgery
droguería	pharmacy
farmacia	pharmacy
farmacia de guardia/turno	duty chemist, late-night pharmacy
ginecólogo	gynecologist

→

médico	doctor
médico general	G.P.
oculista	optician
odontólogo	dentist
otorrinolaringólogo	ear, nose and throat specialist
pediatra	pediatrician
primeros auxilios	first-aid centre
sala de espera	waiting room
urgencias	emergencies

THINGS YOU'LL HEAR

Tome usted ... pastillas cada vez
Take ... pills/tablets at a time

Con agua
With water

Mastíquelos
Chew them

Una vez/dos veces/tres veces al día
Once/twice/three times a day

Sólo al acostarse
Only when you go to bed

¿Qué toma normalmente?
What do you normally take?

Debiera de consultar a un médico
I think you should see a doctor

Disculpe, no lo tenemos
I'm sorry, we don't have that

Hace falta una receta médica para eso
For that you need a prescription

CONVERSION TABLES

DISTANCES

A mile is 1.6 km. To convert kilometres to miles, divide the km by 8 and multiply by 5. Convert miles to km by dividing the miles by 5 and multiplying by 8.

miles	0.62	1.24	1.86	2.43	3.11	3.73	4.35	6.21
miles *or* km	1	2	3	4	5	6	7	10
km	1.61	3.22	4.83	6.44	8.05	9.66	11.27	16.10

WEIGHTS

The kilogram is equivalent to 2 lb 3 oz. To convert kg to lbs, divide by 5 and multiply by 11. One ounce is about 28 grams, and eight ounces about 227 grams; 1lb is therefore about 454 grams.

lbs	2.20	4.41	6.61	8.82	11.02	13.23	19.84	22.04
lbs *or* kg	1	2	3	4	5	6	9	10
kg	0.45	0.91	1.36	1.81	2.27	2.72	4.08	4.53

TEMPERATURE

To convert Celsius degrees into Fahrenheit, the accurate method is to multiply the °C figure by 1.8 and add 32. Similarly, to convert °F to °C, subtract 32 from the °F figure and divide by 1.8.

°C	-10	0	5	10	20	30	36.9	40	100
°F	14	32	41	50	68	86	98.4	104	212

LIQUIDS

A litre is about 1.75 pints; a gallon is roughly 4.5 litres.

gals	0.22	0.44	1.10	2.20	4.40	6.60	11.00
gals *or* litres	1	2	5	10	20	30	50
litres	4.54	9.10	22.73	45.46	90.92	136.40	227.30

TYRE PRESSURES

lb/sq in	18	20	22	24	26	28	30	33
kg/sq cm	1.3	1.4	1.5	1.7	1.8	2.0	2.1	2.3

MINI-DICTIONARY

Where two forms of nouns or pronouns are given in the Spanish, the first is masculine and the second feminine, e.g. 'they' ellos/ellas, 'this one' éste/ésta.

There are two verbs 'to be' in Spanish: ser is generally used to describe people and things (e.g. 'he is a doctor' es médico); estar is used to situate things, i.e. answer the question 'where?' (e.g. 'the station is in the main square' la estación está en la plaza mayor) or to describe a temporary condition (e.g. 'he is tired' está cansado). Both forms are given in this order in the dictionary.

a un/una *(see page 6)*
about: about 16 alrededor de dieciséis
accelerator el acelerador
accident el accidente
accommodation el alojamiento
ache el dolor
adaptor el adaptador
address la dirección
adhesive el pegamento
aeroplane el avión
after ... después de ...
aftershave el after-shave
again otra vez
against contra
agency la agencia
Aids el Sida
air el aire
air-conditioning el aire condicionado
airline la compañía aérea
airplane el avión
airport el aeropuerto
airport bus el autobús del aeropuerto
aisle el pasillo
alarm clock el despertador
alcohol el alcohol
all todo
   all the streets todas las calles
   that's all eso es todo

alligator el caimán
almost casi
alone solo
already ya
altitude: at high altitude en altura
always siempre
am: I am soy/estoy
Amazon: the Amazon Amazonas
ambulance la ambulancia
America Norteamérica
American *(man)* el norteamericano
   (woman) la norteamericana
   (adj) norteamericano
and y; *(before word beginning with 'i' or 'hi')* e
Andes los Andes, la sierra andina
ankle el tobillo
annoy molestar
another otro
anti-freeze el anticongelante
antiseptic el antiséptico
apartment el departamento
aperitif el aperitivo
appetite el apetito
apple la manzana
application form la solicitud
appointment la cita
apricot el albaricoque

are: you are es/está
  (familiar) eres/estás
  we are somos/estamos
  they are son/están
Argentina Argentina
Argentinian *(adj)* argentino
arm el brazo
arrive llegar
art el arte
art gallery la galería de arte
artist el/la artista
as: as soon as possible lo antes posible
ashtray el cenicero
asleep: he's asleep está dormido
aspirin la aspirina
at: at the post office en Correos
  at night por la noche
  at 3 o'clock a las tres
Atlantic Ocean el Océano Atlántico
attractive lindo
  (offer) atractivo
aunt la tía
Australia Australia
Australian *(man)* el australiano
  (woman) la australiana
  (adj) australiano
automatic automático
automatic teller el cajero automático
away: is it far away? ¿está lejos?
  go away! ¡lárguese!
awful horrible
axe el hacha
axle el eje

baby el bebé, el tierno *(CAm)*,
  la guagua *(Chi, Per)*
back *(not front)* la parte de atrás
  (part of body) la espalda
  to come/go back regresar
backpack la mochila
bacon el jamón, el tocino *(Mex)*
  bacon and eggs huevos fritos con
  jamón

bad malo
bag la bolsa
baggage el equipaje
baggage check la consigna
bait el cebo
bake cocer al horno
bakery la panadería
  (selling cakes) la pastelería
balcony el balcón
ball la pelota
banana el plátano, la banana
band *(musicians)* la banda
bandage el vendaje
Bandaid® la tirita
bank el banco
banknote el billete de banco
bar *(drinks)* el bar
  bar of chocolate una tableta de
  chocolate
barbecue la barbacoa
barber's shop la peluquería
  (de hombres)
bargain la ganga
basement el sótano
basin *(sink)* la fregadera
basket la canasta
bath el baño, la tina *(Mex)*
  (tub) la bañera, la tina
  to have a bath tomar un baño
bathroom el *(cuarto de)* baño
battery *(car)* la batería
  (torch etc) la pila
beach la playa
beach ball el balón de playa
beans los frijoles, los porotos
  (Chi, Arg, Uru)
beard la barba
beautiful hermoso
because porque
bed la cama
bed linen la ropa de cama
bedroom la recámara, el dormitorio
beef la carne de res, la carne de vaca
beer la cerveza, el chop *(Chi)*

before ... antes de ...
beginner un/una principiante
behind ... detrás de ...
beige beige
below ... debajo de ...
belt el cinturón
beside al lado de
best (el) mejor
better mejor
between ... entre ...
bicycle la bicicleta
big grande
bill la cuenta
bill (*UK: banknote*) el billete de banco
billfold la cartera
bin liner la bolsa de basura
bird el pájaro
Biro® la lapicera
birthday el cumpleaños
   happy birthday! ¡felicidades!,
   ¡feliz cumpleaños!
birthday present el regalo de
   cumpleaños
biscuit la galleta
bite (*noun: by dog*) la mordedura
   (*by insect, snake*) la picadura
   (*verb: by dog*) morder
   (*by insect, snake*) picar
bitter amargo
black negro
blackberries las moras
blackcurrants las grosellas negras
blanket la cobija, la manta, la frazada
   (*Mex, Ven, Chi, CAm*)
bleach (*noun*) la lejía
blind (*cannot see*) ciego
blinds las persianas
blister una ampolla
blizzard la ventisca
block (*in city*) la cuadra
blond(e) (*adj*) rubio, guero (*Mex*),
   catire (*Cub, Ven, Col*), chele (*CAm*)
blood la sangre
blouse la blusa
120

blue azul
boat el barco
   (*small*) la barca
body el cuerpo
boil (*of water*) hervir
   (*egg etc*) cocer
Bolivia Bolivia
Bolivian (*adj*) boliviano
bolt (*noun: on door*) el candado
   (*verb*) echar el candado
bone el hueso
bonnet (*car*) el capó, el capote,
   el cofre (*Mex*)
book (*noun*) el libro
   (*verb*) reservar
bookstore la librería
boot (*footwear*) la bota
   (*car*) el maletero, la maleta, la cajuela
   (*Mex*), el baúl (*Per*)
border el borde
   (*between countries*) la frontera
boring aburrido, pesado
born: I was born in ... nací en ...
both: both of them los dos
   both of us los dos
   both ... and ... tanto ... como ...
bottle la botella
bottle-opener el destapador
bottom el fondo
   (*part of body*) el trasero
bowl el tazón, la palangana (*Arg, Uru*)
box la caja
box office la taquilla
boy el chico, el joven, el chavo (*Mex*),
   el chaval (*CAm*), el pibe (*Arg*)
boyfriend el novio
bra el sostén
bracelet la pulsera
brake (*noun*) el freno
   (*verb*) frenar
brandy el coñac
brassiere el sostén
Brazil Brasil
Brazilian (*adj*) brasileño

bread el pan
break (*verb*) romper
breakdown (*car*) una descompostura, una pana
  I've had a breakdown se me ha descompuesto el auto/el carro (*Mex*)
breakfast el desayuno
breathe respirar
bribe una coima, una mordida (*Mex*)
bridge (*over river etc*) el puente
briefcase la cartera
British británico
brochure el folleto
broken roto
brooch el broche
brother el hermano
brown (*colour*) café
  (*hair, skin*) moreno
bruise el moretón
brush (*noun: hair*) el cepillo del pelo
  (*paint*) la brocha
  (*for cleaning*) el cepillo
  (*broom*) la escoba
  (*verb: hair*) cepillar el pelo
bucket el cubo, el balde
building el edificio
bumper el parachoques, la defensa (*Mex*)
bureau de change el cambio (de divisas)
burglar el ladrón
burn (*noun*) la quemadura
  (*verb: something*) quemar
  (*of fire*) arder
bus el autobús
  (*long-distance*) el ómnibus, la góndola (*Chi*)
  (*local*) el camión (*Mex*), la camioneta (*Gua*), el guagua (*Cub*), la micro (*Chi*), la buseta (*Col, Ecu*)
business el negocio
  it's none of your business no es asunto suyo
bus station la central de autobuses, la terminal de autobuses

busy (*occupied*) ocupado
  (*bar*) concurrido
but pero
butcher's shop la carnicería
butter la mantequilla, la manteca (*Arg, Uru*)
button el botón
buy comprar
buzzard la águila ratonera
by: by the window junto a la ventana
  by Friday para el viernes
  by myself solo
  written by ... escrito por ...
  by bus en autobús

cabbage el repollo
cable car el teleférico, el funicular
cactus el cacto
café el café
cagoule el chubasquero
cake (*small*) el pastel, el queque (*Chi, Per*)
  (*large*) la tarta
  sponge cake el bizcocho, el panqué (*Col, Ven*)
calculator la calculadora
call: what's it called? ¿cómo se llama?
camcorder la videocámara
camera la cámara, la máquina (de fotos)
campsite el camping
camshaft el árbol de levas
can (*tin*) la lata, el bote, el tarro (*Chi*)
can: can you ...? ¿puede ...?
  I can't ... no puedo ...
Canada el Canadá
Canadian el/la canadiense
  (*adj*) canadiense
canal el canal
candle la vela
candy el dulce
can-opener el abrelatas
canyon el cañón

cap *(bottle)* el tapón
   (hat) la gorra, el gorro
Cape Horn el Cabo de Hornos
car el auto, el automóvil, el carro *(Mex)*
caravan la caravana, el tráiler
carbonated con gas
carburettor el carburador
card *(credit card etc)* la tarjeta
cardigan el cárdigan
careful cuidadoso, cauteloso
   be careful! ¡cuidado!
caretaker el portero, el/la conserje
Caribbean: the Caribbean el Caribe
carpet la alfombra
   (fitted) la moqueta
carriage *(of train)* el vagón
carrot la zanahoria
carry-cot el capazo
case *(suitcase)* la maleta
cash *(verb)* cobrar
   in cash en efectivo
   to pay cash pagar al contado
cash dispenser el cajero automático
cassette el cassette, la cinta
cassette player el cassette
castle el castillo
cat el gato
cathedral la catedral
Catholic *(adj)* católico
cauliflower la coliflor
cave la cueva
cemetery el cementerio
central heating la calefacción central
centre el centro
certificate el certificado
chair la silla
change *(noun: money)* el suelto,
   el sencillo
   (verb: money) cambiar
   (clothes) cambiarse
   (trains etc) hacer transbordo, hacer
   correspondencia
cheap barato
check *(verb)* revisar

check *(noun: bill)* la cuenta
   (money) el cheque
checkbook el libro de cheques,
   la chequera
check-in *(desk)* la (mesa de) facturación
check in presentarse en la facturación
cheers! *(toast)* ¡salud!
cheese el queso
chemist's la farmacia
cheque el cheque
cheque book el libro de cheques,
   la chequera
cheque card la tarjeta de banco
cherry la cereza
   black cherry la guinda
chess el adjedrez
chest *(part of body)* el pecho
   (furniture) el arcón
chewing gum el chicle
chicken el pollo, la gallina
child el niño
   (female) la niña
children los niños
Chile Chile
Chilean *(adj)* chileno
chilli el ají, el chile *(Mex, CAm)*,
   el locoto *(Bol, Per)*
china la porcelana
chips las papas fritas
chocolate el chocolate
   box of chocolates una caja de
   bombones
chop *(noun: meat)* la chuleta
   (verb: cut) cortar
Christian name el nombre de pila
church la iglesia
cigar el puro
cigarette el cigarro
cinema el cine
city la ciudad
city centre el centro (urbano)
class la clase
classical music la música clásica
clean *(adj)* limpio

clear claro
clever listo
cling film el plástico para
  envolver
clock el reloj
close *(near)* cerca
  (stuffy) sofocante
  (verb) cerrar
closed cerrado
clothes la ropa
coach el autobús, el ómnibus,
  la góndola *(Chi)*
  (of train) el vagón
coat el abrigo
coathanger la percha
cockroach la cucaracha
coconut el coco
coffee el café
coin la moneda
cold *(illness)* un resfriado
  (adj) frío
  I have a cold estoy resfriado
  I am cold tengo frío
collar el cuello
  (of animal) el collar
collection *(stamps etc)* la colección
  (postal) la recogida
Colombia Colombia
Colombian *(adj)* colombiano
colour el color
colour film la película en color
comb *(noun)* el peine
  (verb) peinar
come venir
  I come from ... soy de ...
  we came last week llegamos la
  semana pasada
  come here! ¡acérquese!
compact disc el disco compacto
compartment el compartimento
complicated complicado
computer la computadora
concert el concierto
conditioner *(hair)* el acondicionador

condoms los preservativos, los condones
condor el cóndor
congratulations! ¡felicidades!
consulate el consulado
contact lenses las lentes de contacto
contraceptive el anticonceptivo
cook *(noun)* el cocinero
  (female) la cocinera
  (verb) cocinar
cooker la cocina, el horno
cookie la galleta
cooking utensils los utensilios de cocina
cool fresco
cork el corcho
corkscrew el sacacorchos
corner *(of street)* la esquina
  (of room) el rincón
corridor el pasillo
cosmetics los cosméticos
cost *(verb)* costar, valer
  what does it cost? ¿cuánto
  cuesta/vale?
Costa Rica Costa Rica
Costa Rican *(adj)* costarricense
cotton el algodón
cotton wool el algodón
cough *(noun)* la tos
  (verb) toser
country *(state)* el país
  (not town) el campo
cousin el primo
  (female) la prima
crab el cangrejo, la jaiba
cramp el calambre
crayfish las cigalas
cream la crema
credit card la tarjeta de crédito
crisps las patatas fritas
crocodile el caimán
crowded lleno de gente
cruise el crucero
crutches las muletas
cry *(weep)* llorar
  (shout) gritar

Cuba Cuba
Cuban (adj) cubano
cucumber el pepino
cufflinks los gemelos
cup la taza
cupboard el armario
curtain la cortina
customs la aduana
cut (noun) la cortadura
    (verb) cortar

dad papá
damp húmedo
dance (noun) el baile
    (verb) bailar
dangerous peligroso
dark oscuro
    dark blue azul oscuro
daughter la hija
day el día
dead muerto
deaf sordo
dear (expensive) caro
deckchair la tumbona
deep profundo
delayed demorado, atrasado
deliberately a propósito
dentist el/la dentista
deny negar
deodorant el desodorante
department store los grandes almacenes
departure la salida
departure lounge la sala de pasajeros
desert el desierto
develop (film) revelar
diamond el diamante
diaper el pañal
diarrhoea la diarrea
diary la agenda
dictionary el diccionario
die morir

diesel, diesel oil el diesel, el gasoil
    (Ven), el petróleo (Arg)
    (adj) diesel
different distinto
    that's different! ¡eso es otra cosa!
    I'd like a different one quisiera otro
    distinto
difficult difícil
dining room el comedor
dinner (evening meal) la cena
directory (telephone) la guía telefónica
dirty sucio
disabled minusválido
disposable diapers, disposable
    nappies pañales desechables
distributor (car) el distribuidor
divorced divorciado
do hacer
    how do you do? ¿cómo le va?
doctor el/la médico
document el documento
dog el perro
doll la muñeca
dollar el dólar
Dominican (adj) dominicano
Dominican Republic República
    Dominicana
donkey el burro
door la puerta
double room el cuarto doble
doughnut la dona
down abajo
    (downwards) hacia abajo
downstairs abajo
dress el vestido
drink (noun) la bebida
    (verb) beber, tomar
    would you like a drink? ¿quiere
    tomar algo?
drinking water agua potable
drive (verb) manejar
driver el chofer

driving licence, driver's license
el carnet de conducir, el permiso de
conducir, el breve *(Per, Col)*
drunk borracho
dry seco
dummy *(for baby)* el chupete
during durante
dustbin el balde de la basura
duster el trapo del polvo
duty-free libre de impuestos
duty-free shop el duty-free
duvet el edredón

each *(every)* cada
300 pesos each trescientos pesos
cada uno
ear *(inner)* el oído
(outer) la oreja
early pronto
earrings los aretes
earthquake el temblor, el terremoto
east el oriente, el este
easy fácil
eat comer
Ecuador Ecuador
Ecuadorian *(adj)* ecuatoriano
egg el huevo, el blanquillo *(CAm)*
either: either of them cualquiera de
los dos
either ... or ... o ... o bien ...
elastic elástico
elbow el codo
electric eléctrico
electricity la electricidad
elevator el ascensor, el elevador
El Salvador El Salvador
El Salvadorean *(adj)* salvadoreño
else: something else otra cosa
someone else otra persona
somewhere else en otra parte
embarrassing avergonzante, penoso
(Mex), violento *(Arg)*
embassy la embajada

embroidery el bordado
emergency la emergencia
emergency brake *(on train)* el freno de
emergencia
emergency exit la salida de emergencia
empty vacío
end *(noun)* el final, el fin
(verb) terminar
engaged *(couple)* comprometido
(occupied) ocupado
engine *(motor)* el motor
England Inglaterra
English inglés
Englishman el inglés
Englishwoman la inglesa
enlargement la ampliación
enough bastante, suficiente
entertainment las diversiones
entrance la entrada
envelope el sobre
eraser la goma *(de borrar)*
escalator la escalera mecánica
especially sobre todo
evening la tarde
every cada
every day todos los días
everyone todos
everything todo
everywhere en todas partes
example el ejemplo
for example por ejemplo
excellent excelente
excess baggage exceso de equipaje
exchange *(verb)* cambiar
exchange rate el tipo de cambio
excursion la excursión, el paseo
excuse me! *(to get attention)* ¡oiga, por
favor!
(when sneezing etc) ¡disculpe!
excuse me, please *(to get past)* ¿con
permiso?
exit la salida
expensive caro
extension lead el cable alargador

eye el ojo
eyeglasses los anteojos

face la cara
faint (*unclear*) tenue
 (*verb*) desmayarse
fair (*noun*) la feria
 it's not fair no es justo
false teeth la dentadura postiza
family la familia
fan (*ventilator*) el ventilador
 (*handheld*) el abanico
 (*enthusiast*) el fanático
 (*football*) el hincha
fantastic fantástico
far lejos
 how far is it to ...? ¿cuánto hay de
 aquí a ...?
fare el pasaje
farm (*large*) la hacienda, la estancia
 (*Arg, Uru*)
 (*small*) la finca, el rancho (*Mex*),
 la chacra (*Arg*)
fashion la moda
fast rápido
fat (*person*) gordo
 (*on meat etc*) la grasa
father el padre
faucet la llave
fax (*noun*) el fax
 (*verb: document*) enviar por fax
feel (*touch*) tocar
 I feel hot tengo calor
 I feel like ... me apetece ...
 I don't feel well no me encuentro
 bien
felt-tip pen el rotulador
fence la cerca
ferry el ferry
festival la fiesta
fever la fiebre, la calentura
fiancé el prometido
fiancée la prometida

field el campo
fig el higo
filling (*in tooth*) el empaste
 (*in sandwich, cake*) el relleno
film la película
filter el filtro
filter papers los papeles de filtro
finger el dedo
fire el fuego
 (*blaze*) el incendio
fire extinguisher el extintor
fireworks los fuegos artificiales
first primero
first aid primeros auxilios
first floor (*UK*) el segundo piso
first floor (*US*) el primer piso
fish el pez
 (*food*) el pescado
fishing la pesca
 to go fishing ir a pescar
fish shop la pescadería
fizzy con gas
flag la bandera
flash (*camera*) el flash
flashlight la linterna
flat (*apartment*) el departamento
 (*level*) plano
flavour el sabor
flea la pulga
flight el vuelo
floor el suelo
 (*storey*) el piso
flour la harina
flower la flor
flute la flauta
 (*wooden etc*) la quena
fly (*noun: insect*) la mosca
 (*verb: of plane, insect*) volar
 (*of person*) viajar en avión
fog la niebla
folk music la música folklórica
food la comida
food poisoning la intoxicación
 alimenticia

foot el pie
football *(game)* el fútbol
 (ball) el balón
for: for me para mí
 what for? ¿para qué?
 for a week *(para)* una semana
foreigner el extranjero
 (female) la extranjera
foreign exchange el cambio (de divisas)
forest el bosque
 (tropical) la selva
forget olvidar
fork *(for food)* el tenedor
fortnight la quincena
fourth cuarto
free *(not engaged)* libre
 (no charge) gratis
freeway la autopista
freezer el congelador
French francés
French fries las papas fritas
friend el amigo
 (female) la amiga
friendly amable
fringe *(hair)* el flequillo
front: in front of ... delante
 de ...
frost la escarcha
fruit la fruta
fruit juice el jugo de frutas
fry freír
frying pan la sartén
full lleno
 I'm full *(up)* estoy lleno
full board pensión completa
funny divertido
 (odd) raro
furniture los muebles

garage *(for repairs)* el taller, el garaje
 (for petrol) la gasolinera, el grifo *(Per)*
 (for parking) el garage, la cochera *(Mex)*
garbage la basura

garbage can el balde de la
 basura
garden el jardín
garlic el ajo
gas *(UK: petrol)* la gasolina
gas-permeable lenses las lentes de
 contacto semi-rígidas
gas station la gasolinera
gate la puerta
 (at airport) la puerta de embarque
gay gay
gear lever la palanca de velocidades
gel *(for hair)* el gel
gents *(toilet)* los servicios de hombres
German alemán
get *(fetch)* traer
 have you got ...? ¿tiene ...?
 to get the train tomar el tren
get back: we get back tomorrow
 mañana estaremos de regreso
 to get something back recobrar algo
get in *(enter)* subirse a
 (arrive) llegar
get off *(bus etc)* bajarse
get on *(bus etc)* subirse
get out bajarse
 (bring out) sacar
get up *(rise)* levantarse
gift el regalo
gin la ginebra
girl la chica, la joven, la chavala *(CAm)*,
 la chava *(Mex)*, la piba *(Arg)*
girlfriend la novia
give dar
glad contento
glass *(material)* el vidrio
 (tumbler) el vaso
 (wine glass) la copa
glasses los anteojos, las gafas
gloss prints las copias con brillo
gloves los guantes
glue el pegamento
go ir
gold el oro

good bueno
  good! ¡bien!
goodbye adiós, hasta luego
government el gobierno
granddaughter la nieta
grandfather el abuelo
grandmother la abuela
grandparents los abuelos
grandson el nieto
grapes las uvas
grass la hierba
Great Britain Gran Bretaña
green verde
grey gris
grill la parrilla
grocery store el almacén, la tienda de abarrotes/alimentos, el boliche (*Chi, Arg, Uru*), la pulpería (*Cos, ElS*), la bodega (*Gua, Nic*)
ground floor el primer piso
groundsheet la lona impermeable
guarantee (*noun*) la garantía
  (*verb*) garantizar
Guatemala Guatemala
Guatemalan (*adj*) guatemalteco
guide el/la guía
guide book la guía turística
guitar la guitarra
gun (*rifle*) el fusil
  (*pistol*) la pistola

hair el pelo, el cabello
haircut el corte de pelo
hairdresser's la peluquería
hair dryer el secador (de pelo)
hair spray la laca
half medio
  half an hour media hora
half board media pensión
ham el jamón
hamburger la hamburguesa
hammer el martillo
hand la mano

handbag el bolso
handbrake el freno de mano
handkerchief el pañuelo
handle (*on door*) el mango
handsome lindo, guapo
hangover la resaca, el crudo, la cruda
happy contento
harbour el puerto
hard duro
  (*difficult*) difícil
hard lenses las lentes de contacto duras
hardware shop la ferretería, la tlapalería (*Mex*)
hat el sombrero
  (*woollen*) el gorro
have tener
  I don't have ... no tengo ...
  have you got ...? ¿tiene ...?
  I have to go tengo que irme
  can I have ...? ¿me da ...?
hayfever la fiebre del heno
he él
head la cabeza
headache el dolor de cabeza
hear escuchar
hearing aid el audífono
heart el corazón
heater la estufa
heating la calefacción
heavy pesado
heel el talón
  (*of shoe*) el tacón
hello hola
  (*response: on phone*) diga, bueno (*Mex*), hola (*Arg*), aló (*Ven*)
help (*noun*) la ayuda
  (*verb*) ayudar
her: **it's her** es ella
  it's for her es para ella
  give it to her déselo
  her book su libro
  her shoes sus zapatos
  it's hers es suyo
hi! ¡hola!

high alto
highway la autopista
hill el cerro
him: it's him es él
  it's for him es para él
  give it to him déselo
hire alquilar, arrendar
his: his book su libro
  his shoes sus zapatos
  it's his es suyo
history la historia
hobby el pasatiempos
holidays las vacaciones
home: at home en casa
Honduran (adj) hondureño
Honduras Honduras
honest honrado
  (sincere) sincero
honey la miel
honeymoon el viaje de novios
hood (car) el capó, el capote,
  el cofre (Mex)
horn (of car) el claxon
  (of animal) el cuerno
horrible horrible
horse el caballo
hospital el hospital
hot caliente
  (weather) caluroso
  (spicy) picante
hour la hora
house la casa
hovercraft el aerodeslizador
how? ¿cómo?
humid húmedo
hungry: I'm hungry tengo hambre
hurry: I'm in a hurry tengo prisa
hurt: I've hurt myself me lastimé
husband el marido

I yo
ice el hielo
ice cream el helado, el sorbete (CAm)

ice lolly la paleta
if si
ignition el encendido
ill: I feel ill me siento mal
immediately en seguida, al tiro (Chi)
impossible imposible
in en
  in English en inglés
  in the hotel en el hotel
  in Lima en Lima
  he's not in no está
Indian (noun: Native American) el/la
  indígena
  (adj) indígena
infection la infección
information la información
injection la inyección
injury la herida
ink la tinta
inn la fonda
inner tube la llanta
insect el insecto
insect repellent la loción
  anti-mosquitos
insomnia el insomnio
instant coffee el café instantáneo en
  polvo
insurance el seguro
interesting interesante
interpret interpretar
interpreter el/la intérprete
interracial mestizo
invitation la invitación
Ireland Irlanda
Irish irlandés
Irishman el irlandés
Irishwoman la irlandesa
iron (material) el hierro
  (for clothes) la plancha
  (verb) planchar
is es/está
island la isla
it lo/la
its su

jacket el saco
jam la mermelada
jazz el jazz
jeans los vaqueros
jellyfish la medusa
jewellery store la joyería
job el trabajo
jog *(verb)* hacer footing
joke la broma
  (story) el chiste
journey el viaje
jumper el suéter, la chompa *(Per, Bol)*,
  el buzo *(Arg, Uru)*
jungle la selva
just *(only)* sólo
  it's just arrived acaba de llegar

kettle el hervidor de agua
key la llave
kidney el riñón
kilo el kilo
kilometre el kilómetro
kitchen la cocina
Kleenex® los klínex®
knee la rodilla
knife el cuchillo
knit hacer punto
knitwear artículos de punto
know saber
  (person, place) conocer
  I don't know no sé

label la etiqueta
lace *(fabric)* el encaje
ladies' room los servicios de señoras
lady la señora
lagoon la laguna
lake el lago
lamb el cordero
lamp la lámpara
lampshade la pantalla

land *(noun)* la tierra
  (verb) aterrizar
language el idioma
large grande
last *(final)* último
  last week la semana pasada
  at last! ¡por fin!
last name el apellido
late: it's getting late se está haciendo tarde
  the bus is late el autobús se ha
  demorado
later más tarde
Latin America América
Latin American *(man)* el
  latinoamericano
  (woman) la latinoamericana
  (adj) americano
laugh reír
launderette la lavandería automática
laundry *(dirty)* la ropa sucia
  (washed) la colada
laxative el laxante
lazy flojo
leaf la hoja
leaflet el folleto
learn aprender
leather el cuero
left *(not right)* izquierdo
  there's nothing left no queda nada
left-luggage office la consigna
leg la pierna
lemon el limón
lemonade la limonada
length el largo
lens la lente
less menos
lesson la clase
letter *(mail)* la carta
  (of alphabet) la letra
lettuce la lechuga
library la biblioteca
licence el permiso
license plate la matrícula
life la vida

lift (*in building*) el ascensor, el elevador
 could you give me a lift? ¿me podría
  llevar en su auto/carro (*Mex*)?
light (*noun*) la luz
 (*adj: not heavy*) ligero, liviano
 (*not dark*) claro
light bulb la bombilla, el foco (*Mex*),
 la lamparita (*Arg*), el bombillo (*Col*)
light meter el fotómetro
lighter el encendedor
lighter fuel el gas para el encendedor
like: I like it me gusta
 I like swimming me gusta nadar
 it's like ... es como ...
 like this one como éste
lime (*fruit*) la lima
line (*UK: queue*) la cola
 to stand in line hacer cola
lip salve la crema labial
lipstick la barra de labios
liqueur el licor
list la lista
litre el litro
litter la basura
little (*small*) pequeño
 it's a little big es un poco grande
 just a little sólo un poquito
liver el hígado
lizard la lagartija
 (*large*) el lagarto
lobster la langosta
lollipop el chupete
long largo
lorry el camión
lost property office la oficina de
 objetos perdidos
lot: a lot mucho
loud alto
lounge (*in house*) la sala
 (*in hotel etc*) el salón
love (*noun*) el amor
 (*verb*) querer
 I love Mexico me encanta Mexico
low bajo

luck la suerte
 good luck! ¡suerte!
luggage el equipaje
lunch la comida, el almuerzo

mad loco
magazine la revista
mail (*noun*) el correo
 (*verb*) echar al correo
mail box el buzón
make hacer
make-up el maquillaje
man el hombre
manager el/la gerente
many: not many no muchos
map el mapa
 a map of Lima un plano de Lima
marble el mármol
margarine la margarina
market el mercado, la feria (*Arg, Uru*),
 el tianguis (*Mex*)
married casado
mascara la mascara
match (*light*) el fósforo, la cerilla
 (*sport*) el partido
material (*cloth*) la tela
matter: it doesn't matter no importa
mattress el colchón
maybe quizás
me: it's me soy yo
 it's for me es para mí
 give it to me démelo
meal la comida
mean: what does this mean?
 ¿qué significa esto?
meat la carne
mechanic el mecánico
medicine la medicina
medium-dry (*wine*) semi-seco
medium-rare (*steak*) término medio
medium-sized mediano
meeting la reunión
melon el melón
men's room los servicios de hombres

menu la carta
message el recado
Mexican (adj) mexicano
Mexico México
Mexico City la ciudad de México,
el Distrito Federal (Mex)
midday mediodía
middle: in the middle en el centro
midnight medianoche
milk la leche
mine: it's mine es mío
mineral water el agua mineral
minute el minuto
mirror el espejo
Miss Señorita
mistake el error, la equivocación
mixed-race (adj) mestizo
monastery el monasterio
money el dinero
monkey el mono
month el mes
monument el monumento
moon la luna
moped el ciclomotor
more más
morning la mañana
  in the morning por la mañana
mosaic el mosaico
mosquito el mosquito,
  el zancudo (Mex)
motel el motel
mother la madre
motorbike la moto(cicleta)
motorboat la motora
motorway la autopista
mountain la montaña, la sierra
mountain bike la bicicleta de montaña
mountaineering el andinismo
mountain range la sierra,
  la cordillera (Chi)
mouse el ratón
mousse (for hair) la mousse
moustache el bigote
mouth la boca

move (verb: something) mover
  (oneself) moverse
  don't move! ¡no se mueva!
movie la película
Mr Señor
Mrs Señora
much: much better mucho
  mejor
  much slower mucho más despacio
mud el lodo
mug el tarro
mum mamá
museum el museo
mushroom el champiñón
music la música
musician el músico
mussels los mejillones, las cholgas (Chi)
must: I must ... tengo que ...
mustard la mostaza
my: my book mi libro
  my keys mis llaves

nail (metal) el clavo
  (finger) la uña
nail clippers el cortauñas
nail file la lima de uñas
nail polish el esmalte de uñas
name el nombre
  what's your name? ¿cómo se llama
  usted?
nappy el pañal
narrow estrecho
native el/la indígena
  (adj) indígena
near: near the door junto a la puerta
  near London cerca de Londres
necessary necesario
neck el cuello
necklace el collar
necktie la corbata
need (verb) necesitar
  I need ... necesito ...
  there's no need no hace falta

needle la aguja
negative *(photo)* el negativo
neither: neither of them ninguno de ellos
  neither ... nor ... ni ... ni ...
nephew el sobrino
never nunca
new nuevo
news las noticias
newspaper el periódico, el diario
newspaper kiosk el puesto de periódicos
New Zealand Nueva Zelanda
New Zealander *(man)* el neozelandés
  (woman) la neozelandesa
  (adj) neozelandés
next siguiente
  next week la semana que viene
  what next? ¿y ahora qué?
Nicaragua Nicaragua
Nicaraguan *(adj)* nicaragüense
nice lindo
  (place) agradable
  (person) simpático
  (to eat) bueno
niece la sobrina
night la noche
nightclub el cabaré, la peña
nightdress el camisón
night porter el sereno
no *(response)* no
  I have no money no tengo dinero
nobody nadie
noisy ruidoso
north el norte
North America América del norte
North American
  (man) el norteamericano
  (woman) la norteamericana
  (adj) norteamericano
Northern Ireland Irlanda del Norte
nose la nariz
not no
  he's not ... no es/está ...

notebook el cuaderno
nothing nada
novel la novela
now ahora
nowhere en ninguna parte
nudist el/la nudista
number el número
number plate la matrícula, la placa, la chapa *(Arg)*
nut *(fruit)* la nuez
  (for bolt) la tuerca

oars los remos
occasionally de vez en cuando
occupied *(engaged)* ocupado
octopus el pulpo
of de
office *(place)* la oficina
  (room) el despacho
often con frecuencia
oil el aceite
ointment la pomada
OK okay
old viejo
  how old are you? ¿cuántos años tiene?
olive la aceituna, la oliva
olive oil el aceite de oliva
omelette la tortilla de huevos
on ... en ...
one uno/una
one-way ticket el boleto de ida, el pasaje de ida
onion la cebolla
only sólo
open *(adj)* abierto
  (verb) abrir
operation la operación, la intervención quirúrgica
operator la operadora
opposite: opposite the hotel frente al hotel
optician el oculista
or o

orange *(fruit)* la naranja
  (colour) naranja
orange juice el jugo de naranja
orchestra la orquesta
ordinary corriente
other: the other *(one)* el otro
our nuestro
  it's ours es nuestro
out: he's out no está
outside fuera
oven la estufa, el horno
over ... *(above)* encima de ...
  (more than) más de ...
  it's over the road está al otro lado de
    la calle
  when the party is over cuando
    termine la fiesta
  over there por allá
overtake rebasar, adelantar
oyster la ostra

Pacific Ocean el Océano Pacífico
pacifier *(for baby)* el chupete
pack of cards la baraja
package *(parcel)* el paquete
packet el paquete
  (of cigarettes) la cajetilla
  (of sweets, crisps) la bolsa
padlock el candado
page la página
pain el dolor
paint *(noun)* la pintura
pair el par
palace el palacio
pale pálido
palm tree la palmera
Panama Panamá
Panama Canal el Canal de Panamá
Panamanian *(adj)* panameño
pancakes los panqueques
panpipes la zampoña
panties los pantis
pantyhose los pantimedias
134

paper el papel
  (newspaper) el periódico
paracetamol el paracetamol
paraffin el querosén, el queroseno,
  el petróleo para lámpara
Paraguay Paraguay
Paraguayan *(adj)* paraguayo
parcel el paquete
pardon?, pardon me? ¿cómo dice?
parents los padres
park *(noun)* el parque
  (verb) estacionar
parting *(in hair)* la raya
partner *(spouse, friend: male)*
  el compañero
  (female) la compañera
party *(celebration)* la fiesta
  (group) el grupo
  (political) el partido
passenger el pasajero
passport el pasaporte
pasta la pasta
path el camino
pavement la banqueta
pay pagar
peach el durazno
peanuts los cacahuetes, los cacahuates,
  el maní
pear la pera
pearl la perla
peas los chícharros, las arvejas *(Arg, Bol,
  Chi, Col)*
peasant el campesino
  (female) la campesina
pedestrian el peatón
peg *(clothes)* la pinza
  (tent) la estaca
pen la pluma
pencil el lápiz
pencil sharpener el sacapuntas
penfriend el amigo por correspondencia
  (female) la amiga por correspondencia
penknife la navaja
people la gente

pepper la pimienta
　(red, green) el pimiento
per: per night por noche
perfect perfecto
perfume el perfume
perhaps quizás
perm la permanente
Peru Perú
Peruvian *(adj)* peruano
petrol la gasolina
petrol station la gasolinera
photograph *(noun)* la foto(grafía)
　(verb) fotografiar
photographer el fotógrafo
phrase book el libro de frases
piano el piano
pickpocket el carterista
picnic el picnic
piece el pedazo
pig el cerdo, el chancho, el tunco *(CAm)*
pillow la almohada
pin el alfiler
pineapple la piña, el ananás *(Arg)*
pink rosa
pipe *(for smoking)* la pipa
　(for water) la tubería
piston el pistón
pizza la pizza
place el lugar
　at your place en su casa
plains los llanos
plant la planta
plaster *(for cut)* la tirita
plastic el plástico
plastic bag la bolsa de plástico
plate el plato
platform el andén
play *(theatre)* la pieza
　(verb) jugar
　(instrument) tocar
please por favor
plug *(electrical)* el enchufe
　(for sink) el tapón
pocket el bolsillo

poison el veneno
police la policía
policeman el policía
police station la comisaría
poor pobre
　(bad quality) malo
pop music la música pop
pork la carne de cerdo/chancho
port *(harbour)* el puerto
　(drink) el oporto
porter *(hotel)* el portero
Portuguese portugués
possible posible
post *(noun)* el correo
　(verb) echar al correo
post box el buzón
postcard la postal
poster el póster
postman el cartero
post office (la oficina de) Correos
potato la papa
pottery la cerámica
poultry las aves
pound la libra
powder el polvo
　(make-up) los polvos
pram el cochecito
prawns las gambas
prefer preferir
prescription la receta
pretty lindo
　(quite) bastante
price el precio
priest el cura
private privado
problem el problema
protection factor el factor de protección
Protestant *(adj)* protestante
public público
Puerto Rican *(adj)* puertorriqueño
Puerto Rico Puerto Rico
pull halar
puncture el pinchazo,
　la ponchadura *(Mex)*

purple morado
purse (for money) el monedero
purse (UK: handbag) el bolso
push empujar
pushchair la silla de ruedas
put poner
pyjamas el piyama
pyramid la pirámide

quality la calidad
quarter un cuarto
quay el muelle
question la pregunta
queue (noun) la cola
  (verb) hacer cola
quick rápido
quiet tranquilo
  (person) callado
quite (fairly) bastante
  (fully) completamente

radiator el radiador
radio la radio
radish el rábano
railroad, railway el ferrocarril
rain la lluvia
raincoat el impermeable
rainforest la selva tropical
raisins las pasas
rare (uncommon) insólito
  (steak) poco hecho
raspberry la grosella
rat la rata
razor blades las hojas de
  afeitar
read leer
ready listo
receipt el recibo
receptionist el/la recepcionista
record (music) el disco
  (sporting etc) el récord
record player el tocadiscos
136

record shop la tienda de discos
red rojo
  (wine) tinto
refreshments los refrescos
refrigerator la refrigeradora
relative el pariente
relax relajarse
religion la religión
remember: I remember recuerdo
  I don't remember no recuerdo
rent (noun) el alquiler, el arriendo
  (verb) alquilar, arrendar
reservation la reservación
rest (noun: remainder) el resto
  (verb: relax) descansar
restaurant el restaurante
restaurant car el vagón-restaurante
rest room los servicios, el baño (Mex)
return (come back) regresar
  (give back) devolver
return ticket el boleto de ida y vuelta,
  el pasaje de ida y vuelta
rice el arroz
rich rico
right (correct) correcto
  (not left) derecho
ring (to telephone) llamar por teléfono
  (on finger) el anillo
ripe maduro
river el río
road la carretera
rock (stone) la roca
  (music) el rock
roll (bread) el bolillo
roof el tejado
room el cuarto
  (space) lugar
rope la cuerda
rose la rosa
round (circular) redondo
  it's my round me toca a mí
round-trip ticket el boleto de ida y
  vuelta, el pasaje de ida y vuelta
row (verb) remar

rowing boat la barca de remo
rubber *(material)* el hule
  (eraser) la goma (de borrar)
rubber band la gomita
rubbish la basura
ruby *(stone)* el rubí
rucksack la mochila
rug *(mat)* la alfombra, el tapete
  (blanket) la cobija, la manta, la frazada
  (Mex, Ven, Chi, CAm)
ruins las ruinas
ruler *(for drawing)* la regla
rum el ron
run *(verb)* correr
runway la pista

sad triste
safe *(not dangerous)* seguro
safety la seguridad
safety pin el seguro
sailboard la tabla de windsurfing
sailing boat el balandro
salad la ensalada
sale *(at reduced prices)* las rebajas
salt la sal
same: the same dress el mismo vestido
  the same people la misma gente
  same again please otro igual, por
  favor
sand la arena
sandals las sandalias, los guaraches
  (Mex), las ojotas *(Bol, Per, Ecu)*
sandwich el sandwich
sanitary towels, sanitary napkins
  las compresas
sauce la salsa
saucepan la olla
sauna la sauna
sausage la salchicha
say decir
  what did you say? ¿qué dijo ?
  how do you say ...? ¿cómo se dice ...?
scampi las gambas

scarf la bufanda
  (for head) el pañuelo
schedule el horario
school la escuela
scissors las tijeras
Scotch tape® el scotch, el Durex® *(Mex)*
Scotland Escocia
Scotsman el escocés
Scotswoman la escocesa
Scottish escocés
screw el tornillo
screwdriver el destornillador
sea el mar
seafood los mariscos
seat el asiento
seat belt el cinturón de seguridad
second el segundo
see ver
  I can't see no veo
  I see entiendo
sell vender
sellotape® el scotch, el Durex® *(Mex)*
separate *(adj)* distinto
separated separado
serious serio
serviette la servilleta
several varios
sew coser
shampoo el champú
shave *(verb)* afeitarse
shaving cream, shaving foam
  la espuma de afeitar
shawl el rebozo
she ella
sheet la sábana
  (of paper) la hoja
shell la concha
shellfish los mariscos
sherry el jerez
ship el barco
shirt la camisa
shoe laces los cordones (de los zapatos),
  las agujetas *(Mex)*
shoe polish la crema de zapatos

shoes los zapatos
shop la tienda, el almacén
shopping: to go shopping ir de
  compras
short corto
shorts los pantalones cortos
shoulder el hombro
shower la ducha, la regadera (Mex)
  (rain) el chubasco
shrimps los camarones
shutter (of camera) el obturador
  (on window) el postigo
sick: I feel sick (nausea) siento náuseas
  I'm sick (ill) me siento mal
  to be sick (vomit) devolver
side (edge) el borde
sidelights los pilotos, las calaveras (Mex)
sights: the sights of ... los lugares de
  interés en ...
silk la seda
silver (metal) la plata
  (colour) plateado
simple sencillo
sing cantar
single (one) único
  (unmarried) soltero
single room el cuarto individual
single ticket el boleto de ida, el pasaje
  de ida
sister la hermana
skid patinar
skin cleanser la leche limpiadora
skirt la falda, la pollera (Arg, Bol)
skis los esquís
sky el cielo
sleep (noun) el sueño
  (verb) dormir
sleeping bag la bolsa de dormir
sleeping car el coche-cama
sleeping pill el somnífero
slippers las zapatillas
slow lento
small chico

smell (noun) el olor
  (verb) oler
  it smells of roses huele a rosas
smile (noun) la sonrisa
  (verb) sonreír
smoke (noun) el humo
  (verb) fumar
snack la comida ligera
snake la culebra, la serpiente
  (poisonous) la víbora
snow la nieve
so: so good tan bueno
  not so much no tanto
soaking solution (for contact lenses)
  la solución limpiadora
soap el jabón
socks los calcetines
soda water la soda
soft lenses las lentes de contacto
  blandas
somebody alguien
somehow de alguna manera
something algo
sometimes a veces
somewhere en alguna parte
son el hijo
song la canción
soon dentro de poco
sorry: I'm sorry perdón
  sorry! ¡disculpe!
  sorry? ¿cómo dice?
soup la sopa
south el sur
South America América del Sur
South American (man) el sudamericano
  (woman) la sudamericana
  (adj) sudamericano
South Atlantic Ocean el Atlántico Sur
souvenir el recuerdo
spade la pala
Spain España
Spanish español
spanner la llave inglesa

speak hablar
  do you speak ...? ¿habla ...?
  I don't speak ... no hablo ...
speed la velocidad
spider la araña
spinach las espinacas
spoon la cuchara
spring (*mechanical*) el resorte
  (*season*) la primavera
square (*noun: in town*) la plaza
  (*adj*) cuadrado
staircase la escalera
stairs las escaleras
stamp la estampilla, el timbre (*Mex*)
stapler la grapadora
star la estrella
start (*noun: beginning*) el principio
  (*verb*) empezar, comenzar
station la estación
statue la estatua
steak el filete
steal robar
  it's been stolen lo llevaron
steamer (*boat*) el vapor
still todavía, aún
  (*not fizzy*) sin gas
stockings las medias
stomach el estómago
stomach ache el dolor de estómago
stop (*noun: for bus*) la parada
  (*verb*) parar
  stop! ¡alto!
storm la tormenta
strawberries las fresas, las frutillas
stream (*small river*) el arroyo
street la calle
string la cuerda
strong fuerte
student el/la estudiante
stupid bruto
suburbs las afueras
subway (*transport*) el metro,
  el subte (*Arg*)
sugar el azúcar

suit (*noun*) el traje, el terno (*Chi*)
  it suits you te sienta bien
suitcase la maleta
sun el sol
sunbathe tomar el sol
sunblock el filtro solar
sunburn la quemadura de sol
sunglasses las gafas de sol
sunny: it's sunny hace sol
sunshade la sombrilla
sunstroke la insolación
suntan: to get a suntan broncearse
suntan lotion la loción bronceadora
suntanned bronceado
supermarket el supermercado, el super
supper la cena
supplement el suplemento
sure seguro
surname el apellido
sweat (*noun*) el sudor
  (*verb*) sudar
sweater el suéter, el buzo (*Arg*),
  la chompa (*Per, Bol*)
sweatshirt la sudadera
sweet (*noun*) el dulce
  (*adj*) dulce
swim (*verb*) nadar
swimming costume el traje de baño
swimming pool la alberca, la piscina,
  la pileta
swimming trunks el bañador
switch el interruptor, el suiche
synagogue la sinagoga

table la mesa
tablet la pastilla
take tomar
take away (*adj: food*) para llevar
take-off el despegue
talcum powder los polvos de talco
talk (*noun*) la charla
  (*verb*) conversar, platicar (*Mex*)
tall alto

tampons los tampones
tangerine la mandarina
tap la llave
tea el té
teacher el profesor
   (female) la profesora
tea towel el paño de cocina
telegram el telegrama
telephone *(noun)* el teléfono
   (verb) llamar por teléfono
telephone box la cabina telefónica
television la televisión
temperature la temperatura
   (fever) la fiebre, la calentura
temple el templo
tent la carpa, la tienda (de campaña)
   (Mex)
tent peg la estaquilla
tent pole el mástil
than que
thank *(verb)* agradecer
   thanks/thank you gracias
that: that one ése/ésa
   that bus ese autobús
   that man ese hombre
   that woman esa mujer
   what's that? ¿qué es eso?
   I think that ... creo que ...
the el/la
   (plural) los/las *(see page 6)*
theatre el teatro
their: their room su habitación
   their books sus libros
   it's theirs es suyo
them: it's them son ellos/ellas
   it's for them es para ellos/ellas
   give it to them déselo
then *(at that time)* en aquel entonces
   (next, later) luego
there allí
   there is/are ... hay ...
   is/are there ...? ¿hay ...?
Thermos flask® el termo
these: these men estos hombres
140

   these women estas mujeres
   these are mine éstos son míos
they ellos/ellas
thick grueso
thin delgado, flaco *(Mex)*
think pensar
   I think so creo que sí
   I'll think about it lo pensaré
third tercero
thirsty: I'm thirsty tengo sed
this: this one éste/ésta
   this man este hombre
   this woman esta mujer
   what's this? ¿qué es esto?
   this is Mr ... éste es el señor ...
those: those men esos hombres
   those women esas mujeres
throat la garganta
throat pastilles las pastillas para la
   garganta
through por
thunderstorm la tormenta
ticket *(train etc)* el boleto, el pasaje
   (theatre etc) la entrada
ticket office la taquilla, la boletería
tide la marea
tie *(noun)* la corbata
   (verb) atar
tight ajustado
tights los pantimedias
time tiempo
   what's the time? ¿qué hora es?
timetable el horario
tin el bote, la lata
   (material) hojalata
tin-opener el abrelatas
tip *(money)* la propina
   (end) la punta
tire *(noun)* la llanta
tired cansado
tissues los klínex®
to: to England a Inglaterra
   to the station a la estación
   to the doctor al médico**

toast la tostada
tobacco el tabaco
today hoy
together juntos
toilet *(room)* los servicios, el baño *(Mex)*
    (bowl) el retrete
toilet paper el papel higiénico
tomato el jitomate, el tomate
tomato juice el jugo de tomate
tomorrow mañana
tongue la lengua
tonic la tónica
tonight esta noche
too *(also)* también
    (excessively) demasiado
tooth el diente
    back tooth la muela
toothache el dolor de muelas
toothbrush el cepillo de dientes
toothpaste la pasta de dientes
torch la linterna
tour la excursión, el paseo
tourist el/la turista
tourist office la oficina de turismo
towel la toalla
tower la torre
town la ciudad
town hall el ayuntamiento
toy el juguete
track *(UK: platform)* el andén
track suit el chandal
tradition la tradición
traffic la circulación
traffic jam el embotellamiento
trailer el remolque
trailer *(UK: caravan)* la caravana, el tráiler
train el tren
trainers los traíners, los tenis
translate traducir
translator el traductor
    (female) la traductora
travel agency la agencia de viajes
traveller's cheque el cheque de viajero
tray la bandeja

tree el árbol
trousers los pantalones
true cierto
    it's true es cierto
trunk *(of car)* el maletero, la maleta,
    la cajuela *(Mex)*, el baúl *(Per)*
try intentar, procurar
tunnel el túnel
tweezers las pinzas
typewriter la máquina de escribir
tyre la llanta

umbrella el paraguas
uncarbonated sin gas
uncle el tío
under ... debajo de ...
underdeveloped subdesarrollado
underground el metro, el subte *(Arg)*
underpants los calzones
underskirt la combinación
understand entender
    I don't understand no entiendo
underwear la ropa interior
United States los Estados Unidos
university la universidad
unleaded sin plomo
until hasta
unusual raro, extraño
up arriba
    (upwards) hacia arriba
upstairs arriba
urgent urgente
Uruguay Uruguay
Uruguayan *(adj)* uruguayo
us: it's us somos nosotros/nosotras
    it's for us es para nosotros/nosotras
    give it to us dénoslo
use *(noun)* el uso
    (verb) emplear
    it's no use *(never mind)* no importa
useful útil
usual normal
usually normalmente

vacancies *(rooms)* cuartos libres, vacantes
vacuum cleaner la aspiradora
valley el valle
valve la válvula
vase el florero
veal la (carne de) ternera
vegetables las verduras
vegetarian vegetariano
vehicle el vehículo
Venezuela Venezuela
Venezuelan *(adj)* venezolano
very muy
  very much mucho
vest la camiseta
video *(tape)* la cinta de video
  (film) el video
video recorder el (aparato de) video
view la vista
viewfinder el visor de imagen
villa el chalet
village el pueblo
vinegar el vinagre
violin el violín
visit *(noun)* la visita
  (verb) visitar
visitor el/la visita
vitamin tablets las vitaminas
vodka el vodka
voice la voz
volcano el volcán
vulture el zopilote

wait esperar
  wait! ¡espere!
waiter el mozo, el mesero *(Mex, CAm)*,
  el garzón *(Arg, Uru, Chi)*,
  el mesonero *(Ven)*
  waiter! ¡señor!
waiting room la sala de espera
waitress la moza, la mesera *(Mex, CAm)*,
  la garzona *(Arg, Uru, Chi)*
  waitress! ¡señorita!

Wales Gales
walk *(noun: stroll)* el paseo
  (verb) caminar
  to go for a walk ir de paseo
walkman® el walkman®
wall la pared
  (outside) el muro
wallet la cartera
war la guerra
wardrobe el armario
warm caliente
  it's warm today hace calor hoy
was estaba/era
washer la zapatilla
washing powder el detergente
washing-up liquid el líquido lavavajillas
wasp la avispa
watch *(noun)* el reloj
  (verb) mirar
water el agua
waterfall la cascada, la catarata
water heater el calentador (de agua)
wave *(noun)* la ola
  (verb) agitar
wavy *(hair)* ondulado
we nosotros/nosotras
weather el tiempo
wedding la boda
week la semana
welcome *(verb)* dar la bienvenida
  you're welcome no hay de qué
well-done *(steak)* bien hecho
wellingtons las botas de hule
Welsh galés
Welshman el galés
Welshwoman la galesa
were: we were éramos/estábamos
  you were era/estaba
  (familiar) eras/estabas
  they were eran/estaban
west el occidente
wet mojado
what? ¿qué?
wheel la rueda

wheelchair la silla de ruedas
when? ¿cuándo?
where? ¿dónde?
whether si
which? ¿cuál?
whisky el whisky
white blanco
who? ¿quién?
  (more than one) ¿quiénes?
why? ¿por qué?
wide ancho
  3 metres wide de tres metros
  de ancho
wife la mujer, la esposa
wind el viento
window la ventana
  (of car etc) la ventanilla
wine el vino
wing el ala
with con
without sin
woman la mujer
wood *(material)* la madera
wool la lana
word la palabra
work *(noun)* el trabajo
  (verb) trabajar
  (machine etc) funcionar, marchar
worse peor
worst (el) peor
wrapping paper el papel de envolver
  (for presents) el papel de regalo

wrist la muñeca
writing paper el papel de
  escribir
wrong equivocado

xylophone *(wooden)* la marimba

year el año
yellow amarillo
yes sí
yesterday ayer
yet todavía
  not yet todavía no
yoghurt el yogur
you usted
  (familiar) tú, vos *(Arg, Uru, Par)*
  (plural) Ustedes *(see page 6)*
young joven
your: your book su libro
  (familiar) tu libro
  your shoes sus zapatos
  (familiar) tus zapatos
yours: is this yours? ¿es suyo esto?
  (familiar) ¿es tuyo esto?
youth hostel el albergue juvenil

zip la cremallera
zoo el zoo

Eyewitness Travel Guides titles include:
Amsterdam · Australia · Sydney · Budapest · California · Florida
Hawaii · New York · San Francisco & Northern California
France · Loire Valley · Paris · Provence · Great Britain
London · Ireland · Dublin · Greece: Athens & the Mainland
The Greek Islands · Istanbul · Italy · Florence & Tuscany
Naples · Rome · Sardinia · Venice & the Veneto · Moscow
St Petersburg · Portugal · Lisbon · Prague · Spain · Madrid
Seville & Andalusia · Thailand · Vienna · Warsaw